Becoming American Women

Clothing and the Jewish Immigrant Experience, 1880–1920

Barbara A. Schreier

Chicago Historical Society

Becoming American Women: Clothing and the Jewish Immigrant Experience, 1880–1920 is dedicated to Richard H. Needham. His spirited leadership and abiding goodness gave us all purpose. He is sorely missed.

This book accompanies the exhibition *Becoming American Women: Clothing and the Jewish Immigrant Experience, 1880–1920,* which was organized by the Chicago Historical Society.

Exhibition Tour

Chicago Historical Society
March 6, 1994–January 2, 1995

Ellis Island Immigration Museum
New York City
March 15–July 16, 1995

National Museum of American Jewish History
Philadelphia
September 10–December 31, 1995

Published in the United States of America in 1994 by the Chicago Historical Society.

©1994 by the Chicago Historical Society.

All rights reserved.

No part of this publication may be reproduced in any manner whatsoever without permission in writing of the Chicago Historical Society.

Acting Director of Publications: Claudia Lamm Wood

Project Editor: Rosemary Adams

Designer: Bill Van Nimwegen

Composed in Isbell Medium and Leawood Book with Goudy Sans initials. Art produced on a Macintosh IIsi with Quark XPress and Adobe Photoshop.

Printed by Ironwood Lithographers, Inc., Tempe, Arizona

Library of Congress Cataloging-in-Publication Data
Schreier, Barbara A.
    Becoming American women: clothing and the Jewish immigrant experience/Barbara A. Schreier.
        p.   cm.
    Catalog of an exhibition held at the Chicago Historical Society. Includes index.
    ISBN 0-913820-19-9
    1. Jewish women—United States—Costume—exhibitions. 2. Jewish women—United States—Cultural assimilation—Exhibitions. 3. Jewish women—United States—History—Exhibitions. 4. Costume, Jewish—United States—History—Exhibitions. I. Chicago Historical Society II. Title.
GTl0.S37 1994   93-40708
391'.089'924073—dc20   CIP

Contents

The exhibition *Becoming American Women: Clothing and the Jewish Immigrant Experience, 1880–1920* was made possible in part through the generosity of:

Distinguished Benefactor
Barbara and David Kipper and Family

Major Benefactors
Mrs. Peter Bing
The Costume Committee of the
    Chicago Historical Society
Josephine B. and Newton N. Minow
Polk Bros. Foundation

Sponsors
Blum-Kovler Foundation
Arie and Ida Crown Memorial
Nathan Cummings Foundation,
    secured by Beatrice Cummings Mayer
Mr. and Mrs. Clyde W. Engle
Joseph and Bessie Feinberg Foundation
The Illinois Humanities Council
Shirley and Richard Jaffee and Family
Joseph Levy, Jr.
The Lucius N. Littauer Foundation
Patrick G. and Shirley W. Ryan Foundation

Guarantors
Checkers, Simon & Rosner
Computer Discount Warehouse
Henry and Soretta Shapiro

Benefactors
Anonymous
The J. Ira and Nicki Harris Foundation
Dolores A. Kohl
La Salle National Bank
Charlotte Newberger
The Pritzker Foundation

Patrons
Helen and Norman Asher
Robert and Mary Jane Asher
Bank One, Chicago
Barbara Bluhm
Broadacre Management Company
Mr. and Mrs. William Brodsky
Capital Guardian Trust
Michelle L. Collins
Continental Bank
Stewart S. Dixon
Camille Chaddick Hatzenbuehler
Mr. and Mrs. Ben W. Heineman
J. B. Charitable Trust
Renee Logan
Tillie K. Lubin and Sara Lee Schupf
Martha Minow and Joe Singer
Mary Minow and James Robenolt
Nell Minow and David Apatoff
Mr. and Mrs. Potter Palmer IV
Mr. and Mrs. William D. Ross
Mrs. Jacqueline Shapiro
Schellhorn Photo Techniques
Carole and Gordon Segal
Herman Spertus
Mr. and Mrs. Simon Zunamon

The following individuals and institutions provided assistance and/or artifacts to the exhibition:

Mr. and Mrs. Richard D. Abelson

American Jewish Historical Society,
   Waltham, Massachusetts

Collection of John and Selma Appel,
   Michigan State University Museum

Ruth F. Appel

Sanford L. Aronin

The Balch Institute for Ethnic Studies

Ann Barzel

Belle Biondi

Boston Public Library

Sol Brandzel

Elizabeth S. Brown

Fran Brumlik

The Carpenter Center, Harvard University

Myron C. Cass

Chicago Jewish Archives/Spertus Institute

Roberta Gottlieb Cogen

Mr. and Mrs. Leonard Cohen

Lois Cohen

The Family of Fay Kanter Cooper

Susan Costanzo

Curt Teich Postcard Archives/
   Lake County Museum, Illinois

Marilyn D. Davis

Dawn Schuman Institute for Jewish Learning,
   Leah Polin

Judy L. Dean and Susan Dean Jacobs

Meyer Dwass

Dr. and Mrs. Herman L. Eisenberg

Ellis Island Immigration Museum

Ruth Fairfield

Jean Feit

Mr. and Mrs. Melvin S. Feldman

Jewel Rosenthal Fishkin

The Forest Group (The Janger Family Collection)

Alan H. Friedman

Julia Mann Gershon, Harry Mann, and John Mann

Elise Ginsparg

Carolyn B. Glassman and Blanche Glassman Hersh

Marilyn Golden

Paula A. Golden

Muriel Golman

Rivka Gordon, Rabbi Samuel Gordon,
   and David Gordon

Annette A. Grafman

Mary Lackritz Gray

Grace Cohen Grossman

Adele Hast

Hebrew Union College Skirball Museum

Esther Hirsh

Immigrant City Archives

Lois and Richard Janger

The Jewish Historical Society of Maryland, Inc.

Jewish Historical Society of the Upper Midwest

Mrs. Anne Slonimsky Kalikow

Rose Davis Kalver

Abraham J. Karp, Deborah B. Karp,
   and Gertrude Feldbaum

Barbara Levy Kipper

Mrs. Harold (Bunny) Kohn

Rhoda W. Korman

Ellis Freda Faktorow Kovsky

Barbara Kramer

Marcia Rustin Kraut

Jack Kugelmass

Fredi Leaf

Edith Lebed

Deana (Mrs. Leo A.) Lerner

Mollie Levenstam

Joseph Levy, Jr.

Library of Congress

Helen B. Lichterman

Blanche Aronin Lippitz

Lynn Historical Society and Museum

Louise N. Mages

Shelly Farber Marks

The Family of Charles and Shirley Marovitz

Betsy Stein Matek

Mrs. Frank D. Mayer

Myrna K. Metz

Josephine B. and Newton N. Minow

Esther Mott

Museum of the City of New York

Museum of Jewish Heritage

National Yiddish Book Center,
    South Hadley, Massachusetts

New York Public Library

Roberta Newman

Northwestern University Library,
    Special Collections

Vivian S. (Mrs. Bernard L.) Pava

Philadelphia Jewish Archives Center
    at the Balch Institute

Jonathan Prude

Nina Reiter

Elaine G. Rosen and Dina Weisman Rosen

Stuart Rosenberg

Eden Rosenbush

Ricky M. Roth

Sarah Miller Rovner

Grace Schechter Rubin

Naomi and William Rushakoff

Frieda and Evelyn A. Russell

Florence G. Schulman

Shirley Silvers

Rebecca Anne Sive

June Sochen

Spertus Museum

Nathanial Stampfer

Gloria Meiselman Stern

Strong Museum

Fred S. Tanenbaum, in memory of
    Esther Korman Tanenbaum

Anna Totten

Thelma Tuber

The University of Illinois at Chicago,
    Special Collections

Michele Vishny

Rose Dick Wandel

Nina Waranke

Carol B. White

Phyliss Willett

Sylvia R. Wolf

Bertha Shapiro Woodman
    and the Trustees of Haverhill Public Library

YIVO Institute for Jewish Research

Margaret Zunamon

Acknowledgments

So many people have made *Becoming American Women* a part of their lives. My greatest debt is to Josephine Baskin Minow, who believed in this project from the beginning. Jo nurtured me along with the exhibition, showing me the vast boundaries of a loving Jewish heart. Her support has been inspirational and her kindness deeply felt.

I am most grateful to all the members of the *Becoming American Women* Development Committee who contributed their time, advice, and support. Under the skillful guidance of Sue Devine, director of development, who was ably assisted by Laura Sevy, co-chairs Barbara Levy Kipper and Stewart Dixon provided enthusiastic leadership. I would also like to thank Barbara for not only her generosity but also for embracing me with her humor and vitality. I am deeply indebted to all of the contributors to the exhibition. Special thanks go to Mrs. Peter Bing and the Lucius Littauer Foundation, whose generous gifts made this catalogue possible. The support of the Costume Committee of the Chicago Historical Society is deeply appreciated. I also extend my gratitude to the National Endowment for the Humanities. The conceptualization of *Becoming American Women* would not have been possible without the award of an NEH Interpretive Research Grant.

Exhibitions are a team process at the Chicago Historical Society, and I thank Louise Brownell, Emily Clark, Myron Freedman, Bonnie Garmisa, Mary Janzen, Pat Kremer, Wally Rein-hardt, Carol Turchan, and Claudia Wood for all of their contributions. Rosemary Adams is a wonderful editor; she cuts through muddy interpretation with a precise eye and kind words. Special thanks are offered to Joanne Grossman and Carla Reiter who helped shape this project in innumerable ways. Joanne has the enviable ability to organize every aspect of an exhibition without ever losing her sense of humor. Carla infused the project with her luminous prose and ready wit. Douglas Greenberg, president and director of the Chicago Historical Society, and Russell Lewis, director of curatorial affairs, wholeheartedly endorsed this project, and their encouragement is greatly appreciated.

I am indebted to exhibition designer Michael Biddle for capturing the spirit of this show. Michael's design eloquently invites the museum visitor to enter a room filled with visual order and lyrical touches. His aesthetic sensibility gives *Becoming American Women* its charm and power. My thanks to Bill Van Nimwegen for his design of this catalogue. The immigrant voices shimmer against his graceful background. The talents of John Alderson and Jay Crawford are visible in the photographs that enrich the catalogue.

To all of the people who shared their stories and their treasured possessions, I offer my thanks. In their memories, they laid open the richness of their past. I am indebted especially to Richard Jaffee, who shared hours of pleasure listening to the tapes of his grandmother, Rose Jaffee. Thanks to Eden Rosenbush for collecting the

ix

oral histories. Her interviews are filled with intelligence and affection. The Ellis Island Oral History Project proved to be an invaluable source of information, and I am indebted to Ann Belkov and Paul Sigrist for their generosity in sharing these materials.

The *Becoming American Women* team benefited greatly from the wisdom and expertise of several consultants. Grace Grossman, Jack Kugelmass, Jonathan Prude, and June Sochen helped us wrestle with the unwieldy issues, and the themes of the exhibition took shape as a result of their efforts. Barbara Kirschenblatt-Gimblett shared her knowledge with her usual warmth and eloquence. Nancy Bryk, Jenna Joselit, and Russell Lewis reviewed the manuscript and encouraged me to think about costume in more sophisticated and complex ways. I am deeply grateful for their help.

Members of the costume department at the Chicago Historical Society offered help in countless ways; I am most fortunate to work with so many talented people. Susan Samek, associate curator, ably shouldered extra work and responsibilities. I am grateful for the assistance and encouragement of Gayle Strege and Christopher Front. Anna Totten, Jan Tranen, Esther Mott, Jean Feit, and Fredi Leaf volunteered their time to assist with the exhibition. The costumes came to life under the talented hands of the conservator, Nancy Buenger. Donna Shudel used life casts to create mannequins that capture the very heart of this exhibition.

I relied on many people to help with the research. Colleen Sullivan, Lesley Martin, Mary Curran, Aurora Ferraro, Roberta Newman, and Nina Waranke showered me with stacks of xeroxed materials after spending long hours in libraries and archives. Their grasp of the complex and subtle aspects of clothing, immigration, and acculturation yielded a treasure trove of material. I offer sincere thanks to all the archivists, curators, and registrars who made materials available to us. I am especially indebted to Dan Sharon, Zachary Baker, Eve Sicular, Kevin Proffit, Norma Spungen, Pam Nelson, Ellen Smith, Virginia North, Marguerite Lavin, Shari Segel, Olga Weiss, Jeffery Aronofsky, and Monique Maas. To the translators, Meyer Dwass, Susan Costanzo, Nathanial Stampfer, Ann Barzel, Hannah Kliger, and Elise Ginsparg I extend my thanks for making the Yiddish materials accessible.

This project was five years in the making and many people offered unwavering support. Heading the list are my parents, Thomas and Doris Schreier, and my brother, Tom, and his wife, Debbie. My debt to Liv Pertzoff is enduring and passionately felt.

And finally, to Cack, I offer my thanks for everything else.

Barbara Schreier

Preface

In 1782, J. Hector St. John de Crèvecoeur published a small but now well-remembered book entitled *Letters from an American Farmer*. Crèvecoeur, a former French soldier, had made a tour of the Ohio Valley and Great Lakes region of the new United States and had settled as a farmer in New York. Although he returned to France permanently in 1790 to participate in the French Revolution, his reflections on America have echoed repeatedly in our nation's past. He wrote:

> What then is the American, this new man? . . . He is an American who, leaving behind him all his ancient prejudices and manners, receives new ones from the new mode of life he has embraced, the new government he obeys, and the new rank he holds. . . . Here individuals of all nations are melted into a new race of men, whose labors and posterity will one day cause a great change in the world. . . . The American is a new man, who must act upon new principles; he must, therefore, entertain new ideas and new opinions.

These oft-quoted phrases are discordant to us because they are so clearly gendered and objectionable on that account. Scholars may argue about whether Crèvecoeur used "man" generically or not, but we must reject his apparent view that the process of becoming American was something that only men experienced. The Chicago Historical Society's exhibition, *Becoming American Women: Clothing and the Jewish Immigrant Experience, 1880–1920*, demonstrates how dramatically Crèvecoeur's

exclusive focus on men missed the point. This exhibition, conceived by Barbara Schreier, the Society's curator of costumes, insists not only on the equality of women's experience but also upon its primacy in the process through which newcomers to these shores became and are becoming American.

Yet Crèvecoeur's question about what an American is remains a compelling one: becoming American is a complicated and emotional transition. For us, understanding that process requires a willingness to consider the affective bonds that immigration to a new country corrodes. It also requires a tolerance for ambiguity and duality, since these are the essential characteristics of the immigrant's experience, perhaps even more for women than for men.

Becoming American Women, which emphasizes explicitly the experience of Eastern European Jewish women, epitomizes the corrosive character of immigration as well as the ambiguity and duality of identity that corrosion can create in those who suffer it. What immigrant to the United States, regardless of her background, has ever been able to retain all the customs and traditions with which she arrived? What immigrant has wanted to? Contrarily, what immigrant has ever abandoned all the customs and traditions with which she arrived? What immigrant has wanted to?

With the exception of African-American women, who came here against their will and in chains, immigrants to the United States have chosen this destination, even if they sometimes came under duress, fleeing persecution or poverty in their native lands. As a result, immigrants were predisposed to surrender some portion of their cultural baggage when they arrived. For Eastern European Jews, this was an even more vivid prospect since circumstances in their homelands virtually guaranteed that they would not be able to return to retrieve either the metaphorical or physical baggage they had been forced to leave behind.

Thus, as this exhibition so poignantly demonstrates, an Eastern European Jew began the process of becoming an American woman even before she left her home in Russia or Romania or Poland or Ukraine. She had to decide what artifacts of everyday life, especially what clothing, she would bring to the new land. These decisions, made in the crucible of religious persecution with the prospect of America still before the immigrant, reveal much about both the people who made them and the hopes they cherished for their new lives. It is these decisions, as well as the many others that immigrants faced upon arrival in America, that this exhibition addresses.

Which "ancient prejudices and manners" would be abandoned? Which would be preserved? Which "new principles," "new ideas," and "new opinions" would the immigrant adopt and adapt as she became an American woman? The exhibition raises these questions through the medium of apparel, that most immediately apprehended of all our cultural expressions. The exhibition does not pretend to answer such questions for all Eastern European Jews, or for immigrants to this country from other places and other times. Nor does it contend that clothing is the only medium through which such choices can be understood. Rather, the show attempts to raise these questions in a way that makes them accessible and that illuminates their profound relevance to Americans of all backgrounds, whether recently arrived or resident on this continent from earliest times.

This exhibition does demand, however, that the reader of this catalogue, like the viewer of the exhibition itself, confront both the anguish and the joy that immigrant women have undergone as they have made the thousands of small but significant choices through which they became American women. In the largest sense, this exhibition is not only about women or Eastern European Jews. It is also about democracy and its requirements; it is about a polyglot culture and its demands; it is about identity and its components.

There is a tension, in other words, between the particularity of the world this exhibition portrays and its more universal character. This tension is itself evidence of the very ambiguity the women whose clothing we exhibit experienced. We each continue to retain, in differing degree, some portion of our best selves that is distinctly attached to the cultural tradition of our ancestors, and yet we have each also abandoned, again in differing degree, some portion of that tradition in favor of our new identity as Americans.

Barbara Schreier's contention that clothing and choices about it particularly reveal the complexity of the acculturation process is brilliantly innovative and, as executed in the exhibition, profoundly moving as well. For the Chicago Historical Society, a quintessentially urban institution, both the subject of the exhibition and Schreier's approach to it are especially appropriate since immigration was an urban experience and the apparel industry was also urban. We are very proud that the exhibition will be mounted in two other important urban venues: the Ellis Island Immigration Museum in New York and the National Museum of American Jewish History in Philadelphia.

As the grandson of two Eastern European Jewish women immigrants, Anna Neuman and Jenny Greenberg, I confess that I feel an especial attachment to this exhibition as well as a heightened sense of the dual identity it documents. I take real comfort and genuine pride in seeing the experience of my grandmothers (or experiences very much like theirs) documented in the galleries of the Chicago Historical Society. The particularity of my reaction, however, does not detract from the universality of the story the exhibition tells. All Americans are, to take a page from Crèvecoeur, new people, and the new ideas and principles that we share bind us not only to our country but, inevitably, to each other.

Douglas Greenberg
President and Director
Chicago Historical Society

פתחו
שערים
ויבא
גוי צדק

פתחו
לי
שערי
צדק

COPYRIGHT BY HEB. PUB. Cº 1909.

Introduction

The idea for this book began with two stories, both written by Jewish women, who left Eastern Europe as girls and grew up as becoming American women. Rose Cohen and Anzia Yezierska wrote about what they knew—the hope for new opportunities, the strains of dislocation, and the struggle for assimilation. Their highly personal accounts encourage our understanding of the turn-of-the-century immigration experience as a constant balancing act between the inheritance of the past and the promise of the future. Their stories also provide a unique look at the newcomers' preoccupation with dress as an especially meaningful instrument of cultural transformation. As they described their efforts to maintain an equilibrium between the push-and-pull tensions of the old ways and the new, Cohen and Yezierska consciously used clothing both as metaphors and markers of change.

In *Out of the Shadows*, Rose Cohen recalls that shortly after arriving in America, she pleaded with her mother to "leave off her kerchief" so that "she would look younger and more up to date." After a protracted struggle, Rose's mother finally consented, even though:

> She had never before in her married life had her hair uncovered before anyone. . . . When I parted it in front and gathered it up in a small knot in the middle of the back of her head . . . I was surprised how different she looked. . . . She glanced at herself, admitted frankly that she looked well and began hastily to put on her kerchief.

Imploring her mother to leave it off, Rose pointed out that when wives look so old-fashioned their husbands often are ashamed to go out with them. Later that night when her father came home, he looked at his wife's uncovered hair, now fashionably styled, and exclaimed:

> "What! . . . Already you are becoming an American lady!" Mother looked abashed for a moment; in the next, to my surprise and delight, I heard her brazen it out in her quiet way. "As you see," she said, "I am not staying far behind."[1]

Opposite: This 1909 greeting card illustrates the idealized view of America that many immigrants cherished.

Right: Some Jewish immigrants favored the traditional clothing of the Old Country, while others embraced American styles. This family wore traditional dress for their studio portrait, which was taken in Chicago.

For Anzia Yezierska, the transforming power of clothing was equally potent, and her words remind us that some immigrants paid a high price for becoming American women. She presents a moving portrait of the emotional costs in her autobiographical novel, *Bread Givers*. At the end of the novel, Sara confronts the ideological conflict between the Old and New Worlds on the occasion of her mother's death. Following the tradition of Orthodox law, the rabbi makes a tear in the garments of her father and sisters. But when he moves forward to rend Sara's clothing, she refuses: "I don't believe in this. . . . It's my only suit, and I need it for work. Tearing it wouldn't bring Mother back to life again." Her parents' friends and relatives condemn her, crying: "Look at her, the Americanerin!" But Sara resists the pressure. The dark blue serge suit that she guards so zealously symbolizes her transformation into a successful, educated, "real American" woman; Sara chooses to disobey "ages of tradition" rather than sacrifice her hard-won independence.[2]

These two books were the beginning of a search. After reading numerous first-person accounts, we began to talk to families about their immigration experiences. As we listened to stories of their first years in America, one clear fact emerged: although Cohen and Yezierska each brought a writer's sensitivity to the subject of clothing and acculturation, their perspective on the importance of dress as a sign of cultural intermingling and sustaining cultural values closely mirrored the experiences of other immigrant women.

We asked first- and second-generation immigrants to tell us about their families and to talk about the years of adjustment. Interviewers encouraged memories of everyday life; probing for facts, we discovered feelings. Initially worried about the distorting mirror of time, we came to see that absolute truths were not the goal of these interviews. As Eli Evans reminds us, "myths are as important in a fam-ily as 'truths,' because "mystery nourishes history."[3] As we tried to unravel the mysteries, we came to understand that everyone had a clothing story. These memories, told over and over again, became almost ritual evocations of the immigrants' journey. Sometimes a whole ensemble, but more typically one garment or even a precious scrap of fabric, would trigger the most powerful emotions. And it is in these stories, that we discover clothing's complex role as the first step towards Americanization.

Below: Sarah Kaplan Silber.

Opposite: Jewish women and children came to the United States in large numbers, revealing the intention of Jewish immigrants to settle permanently.

Consider, for example, the story Shoshona Hoffman's mother told about her trip from Russia to New York City in 1902. Aboard the ship, she opened her trunk to show another passenger her precious cargo. Packed inside was a new wardrobe carefully selected as an appropriate start to her new life in America. The opinion of her fellow traveler was important because this man had previously lived in New York City. Hearing him proclaim, "These won't do in America," she promptly threw the wicker basket and its contents into the ocean.[4] For Shoshona's mother it was better to come empty-handed than to arrive improperly dressed and be labeled a greenhorn.

Other immigrants confirmed that they did not have to wait until they reached American soil to discover either the appeal or the power of American fashion. In letters sent back to the Old Country, relatives and friends spread the gospel of a new clothing consciousness. When Joe Braufman of Lehr, North Dakota, wrote to his mother-in-law Riva Lazar in Romania, he made it perfectly clear that things were different in America:

> I want to inform you I sent money for tickets for second class passage. . . . Also I sent you $50 for traveling expenses. . . . When you get this letter make sure you are ready to go. Don't take any clothing, because when you get here we will not let you wear those clothes. Take only two dresses and a few things to change on the way. And please don't cry, because your eyes are supposed to be healthy.[5]

Why did immigrants seize upon dress as the critical symbol of their migration? What is it about clothing that captured not only their imagination but the essence of their emotional journey? These are complicated questions that must consider many factors, including class, accessibility, and cultural-based notions of consumption; one answer, however, lies in the adaptability of dress and its ability to transcend and alter an image. While the lack of any standardized sartorial "language" frustrates researchers, the immigrant community must have taken great delight in the expressive potential of dress. The shifting semantics of fashion enabled immigrants to adopt clothing for their own purposes and adapt it to their immediate circumstances, creating their own

Left: While women felt the most pressure to be stylish, men also made changes in their appearance. Many Jewish men cut off their side locks and opted for more modern clothing styles.

The Baskin family, seen here at a family wedding, emigrated from Russia in the 1890s.

social boundaries. Once they made the decision to step on the boat that would carry them to the New World, immigrants entered a world of rapid motion. A change of clothes as the first part of the journey had centrally to do with the need, and the opportunity, to enter the mainstream of a new social life. Their appearance and self-image were inextricably linked, and both were in constant renewal.

This book explores these deep and lasting impressions of clothing as an identifiable symbol of a changing consciousness. In this study of clothing and acculturation, Jewish women take center stage. Jewish émigrés were certainly not alone in the emphasis they placed on "looking American"; indeed the potency of dress as a major emblem of assimilation is a unifying theme of the immigrant experience. Japanese "picture brides," for instance, were taken to a clothing store as soon as they landed in America. Their new husbands, intent upon distinguishing themselves from Chinese immigrants, who were con-

sidered unassimilable because they refused to give up their native dress, insisted that their wives dress in Western clothing. One bride described replacing her traditional kimono with fashionable turn-of-the-century dress, wearing, for the first time in her life, "a brassiere and hip pads."[6] Many immigrant women describe American clothing as their first encounter with the "exquisite torture" of fashionable underwear. Similarly, Maria Frazaetti's lament of a different kind of painful tension created by clothing within her own Italian family crosses all ethnic boundaries:

> My children misunderstand me when I advise them what style clothes they should wear. I blame styles and clothes on some of the stuff in magazines and the movies of this country. If I had my way I would like my children to follow some of the old disciplinary laws of the old country. [7]

Yet, unique circumstances surround the migration of Eastern European Jews that are particularly germane to this investigation of clothing and acculturation. Of all the ethnic and religious groups who came to America between the peak immigration years of 1880 and 1924, Jews were the most likely to envision their move as permanent. Forced to live as outcasts in their homeland, Jews came to America for far more than economic opportunities—they came for safety. As the violence, persecution, and rampant prejudice towards Jews escalated in Eastern Europe, the hopes of returning diminished. During this period, over two million Jews left their homes in Russia, Poland, Romania, Austria-Hungary, and Ukraine. Only 2 to 3 percent of these immigrants made the decision to return to their homeland, in contrast to the 56 percent of central and southern Italian immigrants who returned home.[8] The demographics of this wave of immigrants further supports this. It was a migration of young people (70 percent fell within the ages of fourteen and forty-four) and a migration of families. (Almost half of Jewish emigrants were women as compared to other groups in which females numbered only about a third.)[9] As historian Simon Kuznetz concludes, these are revealing statistics. The large proportion of children and women support the intention to settle permanently and preserve the basic family unit.[10] Determined to start a new life, Jews embraced the American lifestyle and American clothing with a devotion, purpose, and zeal that was seemingly unprecedented by other immigrant groups.

Yet the family would be sorely tested by the strains of uprooting. Those who emigrated as children spoke of the relative ease with which they embraced their new home; many of their parents, however, struggled to find a way to live between the Old and New Worlds.[11] Their children, by comparison, worked to integrate these dual forces into a more cohesive pattern. As historian Deborah Dash Moore concludes:

> They constructed a . . . community with supports borrowed from American culture, middle-class values, urban lifestyles, as well as from their immigrant Jewish heritage, fashioning an enduring structure.[12]

Young, single women had more options in America than their mothers had at a similar age. Earning a wage and surrounded by like-minded peers, adolescent Jewish girls often found America's freedoms more tantalizing than the religious observances and traditions that established the daily patterns of their mothers' lives. Although many mothers welcomed the broader opportunities America offered their children, they also feared the disruption such changes would have on the stability of family life.

These differing expectations are a central theme of this book. While many younger immigrants rushed to step outside traditional boundaries and into America's social parade, older women often felt the weight of their remembered past. In some families, clothing became a norm against which parents could measure their children's devotion and dissension. Racing towards assimilation, young men and women often ignored family pressures to adhere to the old ways. And as parents watched their children's manners and appearance radically change, they sometimes expressed the sentiment that they were witnessing the erosion of Jewish culture. It was in the home that shifting nuances of dress touched immigrants on the most personal level, and it was within the family that conflicting values had to be negotiated as two, and sometimes three, generations of women raised in drastically different environments tried to find a common ground as they searched for their new identity.

Other factors argue for a closer examination of Jewish immigrants. Certainly, their dominant role in the garment industry and needle trades led to a heightened fashion-consciousness. Exposed to the latest clothing trends and surrounded by tantalizing scraps of fabric, young working women developed a taste for American

Immigrant women discovered that standards of modesty varied according to the occasion and time of day. Kate Wolens Maremont dressed in the height of evening fashion.

clothing in both substance and symbolism. Moreover, many Eastern European Jews grew up in a religious culture that used clothing to give meaning to their lives. Clothing traditions were part of Eastern European Jews accumulated history, in which *sheitels* (wigs) and *peyes* (side locks) signified an ethnic and emotional bond. Jews honored the Sabbath with special outfits and acquired new articles of dress as an integral part of holiday celebrations. Styles followed a rigid code of modesty, marked important rites of passage, and reinforced the spiritual framework of their lives. Although not all Jews followed traditional customs, these clothing traditions penetrated their consciousness as part of a shared heritage.

In addition, the Jewish immigration experience provides a unique look at the Americanization process from the perspective of a broad range of socioeconomic backgrounds. In his book *Adapting to Abundance*, Andrew Heinze offers compelling evidence to show that Jews came to the United States from all strata of society.[13] For the millions of Jews who came to escape the poverty of the *shtetls* (towns), there were many others who grew up in comfort and relative affluence. For them, the lure of America's freedoms was not economic but rather religious and political. The very diversity of the Jewish population enriches this study of changing identity since responses to the assimilation process varied in degrees from acceptance to resistance.

The decision to focus principally on women is based on the long-standing relationship women have had with their appearance. In both the Old and New Worlds, issues of dress unified women and framed their experience of life separate from men. This is not to say that men were immune to clothing's persuasive and pervasive symbolism. Details of that all-important bar mitzvah suit still linger in many male memories. And many Jewish immigrants did indeed struggle with the differing cultural expectations,

agonizing over the decision to shave off their beards and cut off their side locks. Although defined by Orthodox law as symbols of religious observance, these emblems of piety immediately marked the man as different and foreign. The immigrant who longed to become a "Yankee" had to endure the barber's blade. Yet even though men considered these issues, they did not record them with the same iconographic vocabulary as did women. Sensitized to the nuances of fashion, female immigrants discuss clothing in their memoirs, oral histories, and correspondence as pivotal markers of their

Below: Fannie Neymark sported the upswept hairdo and wasp waist of the fashionable Gibson Girl in this 1907 photograph.

Responses to assimilation pressures varied. Isaac Sabel, below, continued to follow religious traditions in his dress, while the Adler men, right, posed proudly in their fashionable evening wear.

journey and remembered objects of desire. Similarly, contemporary observers did not pay as much attention to male plumage; even when they did, their words lacked the moralistic, beseeching, and often condemnatory tones with which they addressed women. Certainly both male and female immigrants faced internal desires and external pressures to alter their appearance in America; however, the pressure to be stylish fell largely on women's shoulders.

The standards of fashion were far more complicated and precise for women than men at the turn of the century. Female fashion served an expressive function, proclaiming the status of the whole family. While men might aspire to the plain simplicity of a well-tailored suit befitting a successful white-collar worker, status-conscious women had to learn a code of fashion that dictated every stylish permutation. (That these standards were set by wealthy ladies of leisure far removed from the pressures of tenement life only enhanced their

Immigrants discovered that consumption was an important part of American life. In Chicago, pushcarts and vendors lined Maxwell Street, left, while State Street was home to emporiums such as the Boston Store, below.

desirability.) To signal their participation in the new order of modernity and urban sophistication, immigrant women kept a vigilant watch on fashion trends. As a result of this ongoing dialogue with fashion, it is women's dress that becomes the best yardstick of the newcomers' changing manners and mores.

Jews came to America to make a life as well as a living. Leaving behind the familiar compass of cultural traditions, they came to America where the only thing certain was constant change. The overwhelming majority of Jews settled in urban areas. Cities such as New York, Chicago, Philadelphia, and Boston offered the promise of work and the familiar comfort of relatives and *landsleit* (fellow townspeople). Settling into ethnically cohesive neighborhoods, immigrants found reassuring signposts of their European roots. Ghetto streets were a conglomeration of houses, stores, and peddlers carts. In these neighborhoods Jews could buy kosher meat and matzoh, attend synagogue, and purchase Yiddish newspapers.[14] But while these enclaves helped to ease the newcomers' feelings of alienation, they could not dispel the harsh realities of ghetto life. Instead of streets paved with gold, immigrants found overcrowded apartments, noisy streets, and the pressures of acculturation. For some, the promise of *di goldene medina* (the golden land) remained exhilarating. Mina Friedman's memories were "very sweet because of the freedom I had. It was so different than the hard life I had on the other side."[15] But others could not ignore the grim reality of urban life. Like Anzia Yezierska, they found a world filled with "rooms without sunshine."[16]

Many Jews found immigration to be a shattering emotional experience. In her memoirs, Mary Antin asks us to think about the trauma of resettlement:

> Now imagine yourself parting with all you love believing it to be a parting for life; breaking up your home, selling the things that years have made dear to you; starting on a journey without the least experience in travelling. . . . How do you feel?[17]

For women who grew up in a climate of poverty, in houses they described as "little shacks" without floors, the transition was overwhelming.[18] But even immigrants who had lived in Eastern European cities had difficulty adjusting. Before coming to America, Anna Kuthan left her home in Czechoslovakia to work for a family in Vienna. When she returned to her parents' home in Usti Nad for a visit, her parents didn't recognize her because she was "dressed up Modern" in a velour hat and navy blue coat. Her father worried about what people would say, but Anna remained unconcerned. "I say the hell with the people, I come from big city; I have so much experience, I'm no more small-town girl believe me." But Anna's big-city experiences in Vienna did not adequately prepare her for life in America. She found the pace of life so different that she "didn't smile for a long time." Anna explained, "Everybody was for himself and they was always money, money, money, rush, rush, rush."[19]

Given the magnitude of this adjustment and the strangeness of their new home, it is easy to understand why immigrants seized upon clothing as an outward sign of cultural adaptation. Sara Abrams remembered having to learn the words (and the concepts behind them) of "crisis," "shops," and "mind jarownbusiness" from her Americanized uncle.[20] But mastering the language took months, even years; by purchasing a new parasol or refashioning an old dress, the newcomers could quickly make a vital cultural connection to their new surroundings. A hat modeled after the styles on Fifth Avenue, a pair of high-heeled shoes suitable for a Saturday night dance, or even a lacy collar purchased to dress up a plain cotton blouse signaled a changing point of view. Form preceded word, creating a much-needed sense of belonging. In their quest for a new cultural identity, Jewish immigrants marshaled an impressive array of sartorial symbols that connected them to the traditions of their past and the promise of their future.

Once they settled into their new home, the arrivals came face to face with the American value of consumption, a system that prized spending over saving and rewarded accumulation instead of self-sacrifice. It also was a world steeped in fashion. Deeply impressed by America's offerings, they quickly developed an appetite for a new standard of living. Everywhere they looked, immigrants found the visual rewards and powerful symbolism of things and money. Posters, advertisements, and photographs transformed city storefronts into billboards of fashion beckoning with sumptuous garments.[21] A neighborhood stroll on the Sabbath or on holidays became a parade, a public event designed to showcase the latest acquisitions. When they entered American department stores, immigrants encountered palaces of materialism well-stocked with alluring ready-to-wear clothing. The urban street was a scene of exuberant consumerism with overflowing pushcarts and easy installment plans for those with more desire than money. A New York street vendor stripped the complexities of acquisition to its most elemental form in his plaintive, desperate cry: "Women, women want! Please, please want— begin to want!"[22]

From all quarters, immigrants heard the same message—to become American women, one had to look the part. But if the choice was clear, the decision was not without conflict, and it is here, in the consequences of an altered appearance, that the power of clothing is best understood. Many women came dressed in styles that were culturally anchored to their Jewishness, and they found themselves torn between the old ways and the new. When Mary Antin's mother joined her husband in America she discovered that he had abandoned the tenets of Orthodox Judaism. Confronted

with his demands that she follow his example, she acquiesced to his wishes but with great personal pain. "My mother," wrote Antin, "gradually divested herself . . . of the mantle of orthodox observance; but the process cost her many a pang, because the fabric of that venerable garment was interwoven with the fabric of her soul."[23]

Some women learned the painful lesson that Americans established their own code of social rank for newcomers and that assimilation went far beyond material possessions. In Anzia Yezierska's *Hungry Hearts*, Shenah Pessah declares: "There's something in me—I can't help—that so quickly takes on to the American taste. It's as if my outside skin only was Russian; the heart in me is for everything of the new world." Shenah later discovers that the joy she takes from her transformation is premature when the man of her dreams fails to see her as a desirable woman in spite of her new "shining straw hat" and dress of the "greenest, crispest organdie." Accepting his indifference, she acknowledges that "there were other things to the person besides the dress-up."[24]

Other Jews concluded that a change of clothes could lead to a change of heart with disastrous effects. Their Jewish identity, well-defined and reinforced by long-standing clothing traditions in Eastern Europe, suffered from

Young immigrant women had more opportunities in the United States than their mothers had in Eastern Europe. This young woman seeks employment in New York City.

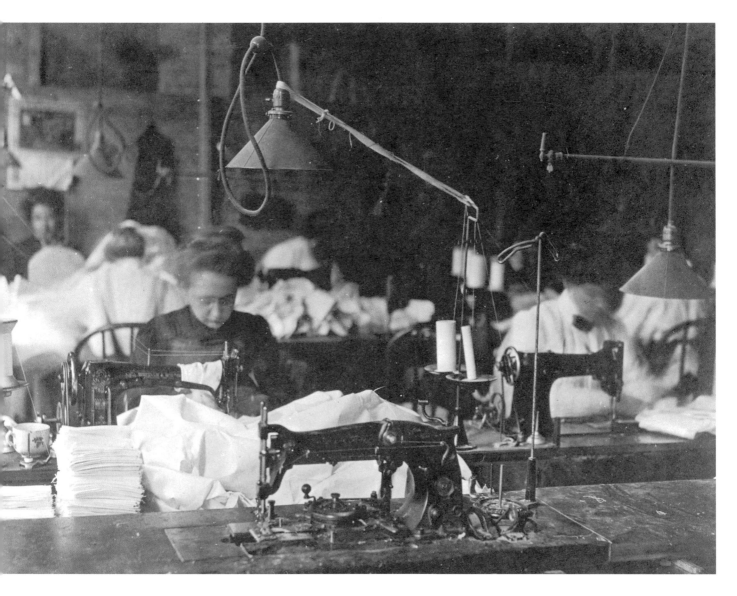

Jewish immigrants dominated the garment industry and needle trades.

the secular contamination of American modes and mores. So eager were they to "throw off the mantle of tradition" that they failed to consider the portentous consequences of their decision.[25] After rejecting the pivotal symbols of religious devotion with which they grew up in the Old World, some found the American dress code spiritually empty.

Yet the immigrant voices that inform this book confirm that the results also offered great joy. Treasured bits and pieces of American style were a profound source of fulfillment. It could be a dress purchased through an installment plan, five-cents worth of silk ribbon from a peddler's pushcart, or salvaged remnants from a cutting-room floor. These items symbolized the new arrivals' transformation and signified that the struggle to come to America had been worthwhile.

Jewish immigrants understood the importance of dressing the part long before they grasped the full impact of their migration. But one should not mistake Eastern European Jews at the turn of the century for semioticists interested in dissecting clothing styles like cryptographers searching for an encoded message.

Nor should it be assumed that they tried to create a separate "language of fashion," that recently cliched notion of a sartorial vocabulary complete with grammar and syntax.[26] Clothing was far more than a cultural footnote in this study of assimilation. Jews consciously used the symbolic richness of dress, widely understood within the immigrant community, as a means to a very specific end. Therefore their clothing choices and the resulting consequences of their decisions enable us to trace the process of traveling from the familiar to the unknown. For Jews carried with them the traditions of their homeland in which clothing symbolism had cultural antecedents, and whether they chose to continue or disrupt the patterns, the memories left an indelible impression. But as immigrants crossed the threshold of a new culture, they had to ask themselves: "How do I fit in?" Adopting and adapting American fashions promised both to appease their anxiety and to secure a successful transition. And once they began their new life, dressing "modern" provided reassurance that the effort was not only attainable, but worthwhile.

Becoming American women implied neither a willful abandonment of everything associated with the Old Country nor an unquestioning acceptance of everything American.[27] The magnitude of change was too great for such a simplistic symbolic resolution. While Ida Richter, for example, longed for beautiful "American" clothes, her mother refused to dress up because "God don't want them to be showoffs."[28] The spectrum of responses contained in this book remind us that there are many ways to redefine and reimage oneself. Ultimately, the decision of how and if to remake oneself came down to personal choice as each woman found her way. Laid out before us, these clothing decisions create a historical mosaic of collective purpose.

After her marriage, Sarah Kaplan Silber chose to cover her head with a stylish American hat rather than a traditional sheitel.

Writing about rituals, religious scholar Micrea Eliade says, "One becomes what one displays."[29] As they began their journey to become American women, Jewish immigrants displayed themselves with promise and purpose.

Notes

1. Rose Cohen, *Out of the Shadows* (New York: 1918), 153–54.

2. Anzia Yezierska, *Bread Givers* (Garden City, New York: 1925; reprint, New York: 1975), 255.

3. Eli Evans, *The Lonely Days Were Sundays: Reflections of a Jewish Southerner* (Jackson, Missisippi: 1993), 13.

4. Interview with the author.

5. Joe Braufman correspondence, courtesy of Helen B. Lichterman. I am grateful to the Jewish Historical Society of the Upper Midwest for bringing this letter to my attention.

6. Emma Gee, "Issei Women: 'Picture Brides' in America," reprinted in Maxine Schwartz Seller, ed., *Immigrant Women* (Philadelphia: 1981), 56.

7. WPA interview with Maria Frazaetti, January 1938, quoted in Elizabeth Ewen, *Immigrant Women in the Land of Dollars: Life and Culture on the Lower East Side, 1890–1925* (New York: 1985), 202.

8. Abraham J. Karp, ed., *Golden Door to America: The Jewish Immigrant Experience* (New York: 1976), 15.

9. Simon Kuznetz, "Immigration of Russian Jews to the United States: Background and Structure," *Perspectives in American History* 9 (1975): 94–100.

10. Sydney Stahl Weinberg, *The World of Our Mothers: The Lives of Jewish Immigrant Women* (Chapel Hill: 1988), xix.

11. Deborah Dash Moore, *At Home in America: Second Generation New York Jews* (New York: 1981), 11.

12. Andrew R. Heinze, *Adapting to Abundance: Jewish Immigrants, Mass Consumption, and the Search for American Identity* (New York: 1990).

13. Edward Mazur, "Jewish Chicago: From Diversity to Community," in Melvin G. Holli and Peter d'A. Jones, eds., *Ethnic Chicago* (Grand Rapids: 1984), 55.

14. Mina K. Friedman, "Time About No News To All," unpublished manuscript, courtesy of Alan Friedman.

15. Anzia Yezierska, *Hungry Hearts* (New York: 1920), 264.

16. Mary Antin, *From Plotzk to Boston* (New York: 1985), 80.

17. Immigrant Labor History Project, I-25, Tamiment Library, New York University.

18. Interview with Anna Kuthan, Immigrant Labor History Project.

19. Sara J. Abrams, "An Autobiographical Family Portrait," unpublished manuscript, American Jewish Autobiographies Collection, #92, YIVO Institute for Jewish Research.

20. Stuart Ewen and Elizabeth Ewen, *Channels of Desire: Mass Images and the Shaping of American Culture* (New York: 1982), 81–82.

21. "A Hayseed in New York," *Jewish Daily News*, March 23, 1903.

22. Mary Antin, *The Promised Land* (Boston: 1912), 246–47.

23. Yezierska, *Hungry Hearts*, 57.

24. Sanford E. Marovitz, "The Lonely New Americans of Abraham Cahan," *American Quarterly* 20:1 (Summer 1968): 206.

25. Fred Davis, *Fashion, Culture, and Identity* (Chicago: 1992), 3–5.

26. Stuart Ewen and Elizabeth Ewen, "Americanization and Consumption," *Telos*, Fall 1978: 44.

27. Ida Richter, Tape I, Papers of Jenny Masur, YIVO Institute for Jewish Research.

28. Micrea Eliade, *Images and Symbols: Studies in Religious Symbolism*, trans. Philip Mairet (New York: 1961).

Di Alte Heym

Small Jewish towns and villages of Eastern Europe were known as shtetls. Traditional religious rituals and customs flourished in shtetls such as this one.

When asked if she ever missed *di alte heym* (the old home), Fannie Friedman, a Ukrainian immigrant replied, "Never. Never. . . . When we left it was just awful. The Revolution went on for some time, and they were killing each other."[1] But for Gilda Hochman, who left Russia at age eleven, the pain of saying goodbye was overwhelming. "There were three wagons going," she remembered. "Ours was the last, and my little grandmother was left behind. I used to take her to the river every Friday. I would put her on a little rock and I would wash her and she would bless me. And I had to say goodbye to my grandma."[2]

The mass migration of Eastern European Jews at the turn of the century was epic in proportion, yet the statistical evidence of this collective movement should not overshadow the individual feelings of hope and despair that accompanied the immigration experience.

Lazarus Salamon, a Hungarian Jew who traveled to America in 1920, eloquently expressed the conflicts of his decision: "I feel like I had two lives. You plant something in the ground. It has its roots. And then, you transplant it where it stays permanently. That's what happened to me."[3] For the more than two million Jews who left Eastern Europe as part of a large-scale migration, this sense of uprooting was palpable.

The world they left behind in the Old Country was, at its very core, a society of faith where people felt connected to a community rather than a country. Surrounded by indifferent and often hostile neighbors, Eastern European Jews turned to each other for sustenance. The cultural ambiguity that emerged once they

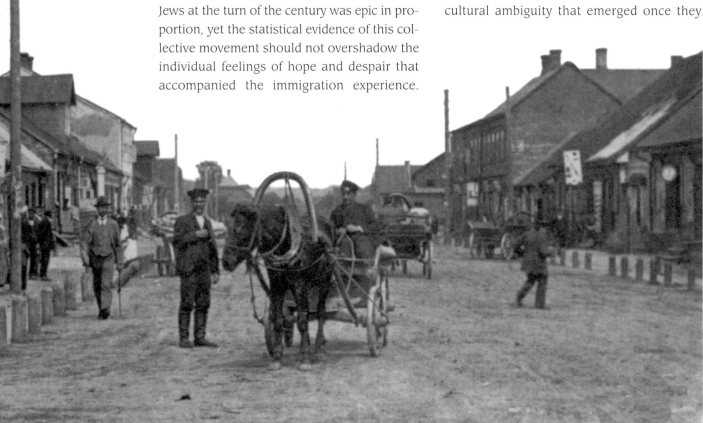

reached America was conspicuously absent in the homeland. While first generation immigrants wondered, "Which am I first, a Jew or an American?" the question of identity was easily decided in the Pale of Settlement. This was an area in western and southwestern Russia and eastern Poland where Jews were forced to live by government decree. In light of the persecution and anti-Semitic actions of the Czarist government, Eastern European Jewry felt few of the ties of nationality; instead they pledged their allegiance to an ethnic and religious identity. Shmuel Goldman felt culture-bound not to the Russian language but to Yiddish, the "language of exile":

> We call [it] the mama-loshen. That means more than mother tongue. It is the *mother's* tongue because this was the language the mother talked, sweet or bitter. It was your own. It is a language of the heart. . . . The language was our republic.[4]

When asked about her feelings about leaving Russia at the age of thirteeen, Ruth Metzger adamantly asserted: "I just wanted to forget it. I didn't even want to speak Russian. . . . We lost eighteen people of our family. So I had a hatred for Russians."[5] Similarly, Mary Antin began her autobiography *The Promised Land* with a description of her attitude towards Russians as "the other": "The world was divided into two parts: . . . Polotzk, the place where I lived, and a strange land called Russia. . . . Russia was . . . far off, and . . . many bad things happened there."[6] Writing the history of Eastern European Jews, Irving Howe described these people as "a kind of nation" without "recognized nationhood."[7]

Life in turn-of-the-century Eastern Europe was in a state of flux, and the world of shtetl would forever be changed. Moreover, the values of religious piety and devotion varied widely among Eastern European Jews. However, this place, with its long-standing traditions and customs, remained the point of departure for many

Above: An Eastern European shtetl. Left: The Lipschultz family in Russia, c. 1910. In Eastern Europe, the family was the center of Jewish life.

Right: Studying at the Synagogue *and* At the Heder *by Ilex Beller. Men have charge of public religious ceremony. Young boys begin as early as age three to attend the* heder, *or Hebrew school.*

Below: Prayerbooks. For the devout, religion permeated daily life.

Jews. Even if it existed only in memory, it is useful to present a snapshot, painted in broad brushstrokes, of a moment in time.

Joined by a common language of Yiddish, connected by communal institutions, and molded by a powerful sense of shared history, many Eastern European Jews grew up in a world where the overarching context was religious. Here customs and rituals followed the law of God as revealed in the Torah, and centuries-old traditions established the rhythms of daily life. In addition to religious life, civil actions, including marriage, divorce, and inheritance, fell within the jurisdiction of Jewish law "as expressed in the Talmud and interpreted by the rabbis."[8]

For the devout, religious observances gave form to each day with the prayers said upon waking to the way one got dressed for the day

and the blessings said over the food at night. These observances also gave form to the week, bringing the family together on Friday night to celebrate the Sabbath. Emanual Kirwin explained in his account of life in Tarnow that the observance of these rituals was not just what you did, it was the "way everybody lived. . . . We didn't know what to be religious meant."[9] Adhering to kosher dietary laws, keeping the Sabbath holy, and reciting the morning prayer upon rising were just 3 of 613 commandments that regulated a Jew's life. Jews sanctified their daily order through regular prayer and rituals, affirming their belief that the spiritual and physical dimensions of life were inseparable.[10] These highly ritualized displays of faith, as often celebratory as obligatory, served a crucial function. Anthropologist Barbara

Synagogues such as this one in Poland were the center of religious life and united Jewish communities.

A washing cup, above, is used in ritual handwashing before the Sabbath meal. Left: Copper pot, cake mold, and mortar and pestle, which Eastern European immigrants brought to America.

Women's breadwinning labor was expected and respected in Jewish society. These women sold goods in the marketplace.

Myerhoff explains it so well: Judaism's particular richness of ceremony and symbolism rendered suffering and scarcity explicable and thus bearable.[11] These patterns flourished in the ethnically homogenous setting of the shtetl; yet even when Jews, either by force or choice, moved to more urban settings in Eastern Europe, they carried with them the values of the shtetl culture.[12]

At the heart of the shtetl community was the family. Valued as the central bond in a person's life, the family was the fixed point of reference; all lines of authority, kinship, and status radiated from this stable center. Living in small one-story wooden homes that lined the main street of the shtetl, families worked and prayed together, retracing the steps of their ancestors.[13] As one immigrant described, privacy was unimaginable in these close quarters, so every act took on a communal dimension:

> Our house was one room—a log house with paper windows. . . . The oven on the one side gave us warmth, and baked the bread for the whole week. On top of it, a few of the children could stretch out at night, and get some sleep, for there was not enough room elsewhere for them.[14]

Each member of the household had specific duties to fulfill, and these obligations powerfully reinforced the differences in male and female roles. Families, like the communities, were divisible by gender. The father stood as the unquestioned head of the household and the spiritual authority figure in the family. Assuming the responsibilities of public worship and religious leadership, men dominated the world of the synagogue. Their sons studied and prepared for this responsibility in the *heder* (elementary religious school) and, when possible, the *yeshiva* (rabbinical academy). As one of the most important pathways to God, scholarship was a highly respected form of worship, and Jewish immigrants often remember education as the crucial distinction between themselves and their Gentile neighbors.[15]

Women were encouraged to integrate the values of the community into the family's domestic realm; many women remember the kitchen as their schoolroom. There, wrote Mary Antin, a girl "learned how to bake and cook and manage . . . and while her hands were busy, her mother instructed her . . . in the conduct proper for a Jewish wife."[16] Prevented from taking an active role in religious services, Jewish women directed their energies to household chores and outside work, dominating both the home and the marketplace. Mina Friedman remembers her grandmother as "the real breadwinner in the family." Twice a year, she would leave their small village of Kislavich and travel to Kiev to "buy a lot of secondhand clothes which she would sell to the peasants. . . . She also kept geese and would sell the goose feathers."[17]

Mina's grandmother was not alone. Jewish women in Eastern Europe played a vital role in the family's economic survival. As a practical extension of their religious duties, women's work was expected and respected in Jewish society. Whenever possible, a woman worked to support her husband's life of religious study; more typically, however, both incomes were needed to provide the basic essentials of food, clothing, and shelter. In either case, a woman's breadwinning labor coalesced with her domestic destiny. Expected to serve as the custodian of the family's financial as well as emotional concerns, Jewish women developed a strong business acumen. This contrasted sharply with the American ideal, which assumed that married status meant retirement from the work force.[18]

Laboring wives and daughters sought every employment opportunity, working as shopkeepers, factory workers, and artisans. They made cigarettes, cigars, and other consumer goods. The majority of women, however, worked in some type of needle trade. Although small by American standards, Eastern European manufacturers began to industrialize clothing production by the turn of the century. Jewish women found employment in the ready-to-wear garment industry, either in factories or in their homes doing contract work. Sewing skills also provided women with a livelihood in small towns and villages. Working as dressmakers and seamstresses, women produced goods for individual customers; the less fortunate crafted cheaper goods, which they peddled in the local marketplace.[19] Neighboring peasants used to come to Fannie Friedman's town of Chechelnic once a week to sell chickens, potatoes, and onions. In exchange, her mother "used to sew . . . for the peasant women."[20]

When Eastern European immigrants recall life in the homeland it is the *bobbe* (grandmother) and the *balebosteh* (householder) who dominate their memories. Collectively they present a group portrait of women who labored for their family's well-being in a precarious environment. Sustained by their faith and supported by their community, married women worked to make a Jewish home. While fathers schooled their children in the world of formal religion, mothers, by word and example, taught them the practical lessons of what subsequent generations would term "domestic religion." One immigrant described shtetl women as the

Many women worked in the garment industry, either in factories, like the one pictured here, or in their homes as dressmakers and seamstresses.

Dora Ruben, right, ran a wheat mill in Russia to support her family. Yetta Weisman, far right, shown with her children, sold notions and fabric in Poland.

family's guide. "Always, it was the woman who gave the moments of life into the family. . . . Uneducated she was, but the woman did the rituals. . . . She knew how to live with all the men prayed and talked about."[21] The organized structure of the shtetl established rigid boundaries for women, yet women's powerful family role is undisputed. Domestic concerns were the issues that touched every life, and these remained the domain of women.

Community and family ties coalesced around the marriage ceremony. This highly patriarchal culture, which defined a woman's status in relation to a man, made no provisions for an unmarried woman. Put simply, marriage gave meaning to a woman's adult existence. To raise a family was to serve God; therefore, marriage and motherhood were the unquestioned goals. Mary Antin recalled that to avoid the "greatest misfortune" of becoming an old maid, "the girl and her family, to the most distant relatives, would strain every nerve, whether by contribut-

ing to her dowry, or hiding her defects from the marriage broker, or praying and fasting that God might send her a husband."[22]

Marriage was the pivotal moment in a woman's life and, like every other religious event in the shtetl, traditional rituals surrounded the occasion. Of primary importance was the bride's first visit to the *mikvah* (ritual bath), which purified her soul. Upon entering the *mikvah,* an attendant greeted the bride and led her to the pool, dipping her into the water three times. Each time the bride emerged, the attendant said a prayer and proclaimed, "This is a kosher daughter of Israel."[23] After this initiation, she would fulfill her religious duties by going to the mikvah after each menstrual period to wash away the impurities of menstruation.

The wedding ceremony was a community affair, concluding months of careful negotiation. Parents on both sides evaluated their child's prospective mate, negotiated a dowry, and then signed a *tnoyim* (contract). A pair of feather pillows, a tablecloth, candlesticks, and dishes were considered the minimum dowry a girl could offer.[24] Romantic attraction was not factored into the careful arithmetic of these arbitrations. According to shtetl logic, "First you marry, and then you love."[25] In some instances the negotiations took place without the betrothed couple ever meeting. Dina Rosen's father used to tell of the surprise awaiting him on his wedding day. Struck by his bride Yetta's shortness, he realized that the only other time he had ever laid eyes upon her she had been sitting down.[26]

When the *kale* (bride) finally stood beneath the *chuppah* (wedding canopy) with her *khossen* (groom), it ideally represented the joining of two families of comparable or complementary status. In the shtetl, money was not the sole, or even the most important, determinant of status. A Jew's lineage and occupation determined his or her ranking and the fixed hierarchical lines created a caste system. A woman who left Bessarabia, Russia, in 1914 at the age of seventeen explained the all-important distinction between the *sheyne* (fine) and *proste* (common) Jews. "Essentially, the *proste Yid* was the one who worked for someone else." Since her parents belonged to the sheyne class, they refused to let her associate with tradesmen's daughters even though her family was poorer.[27]

Family status or *yikhes* was one of the major considerations in arranging a match. A woman who lived in Sandemish, Poland, recalled the unhappy consequences of such status consciousness in her own family. Her sister wanted to marry a "proster Jew," but her grandfather protested. "He claimed that he didn't want a *fleck* (spot) on the family name and if she married this man there would be." Her sister broke off the match with her young worker because "when my grandfather said no, it was no." Instead she entered into a loveless match with a merchant who was from a

The Jewish mikvah is the bathhouse for purifying the spirit as well as the body.

feinereh (finer) family.[28] Unhappiness was not, however, the inevitable fate of such arranged marriages. Morris Cohen, for example, described his parents' relationship as affectionate, based on "the love that grows out of devotedly living together in common efforts."[29]

The most sought-after males were learned men whose family had a high degree of yikhes. Parents seeking such a catch for their daughter often had to offer a large dowry and a *kest*, an agreement to support the couple for a specified period of time while the youth continued his studies. A prospective bride was assessed according to her parents' status and by her own skills and appearance. Kalya Rivkin's future in-laws chose her as a "good risk" for their intellectual son because she had opened her own dressmaking business.[30]

A Wedding by Ilex Beller.

This certificate, right, recognizes the 1901 marriage of Moshe Weisman and Yetta Yoskewiecz. Linens and candlesticks, below, were typical dowry items.

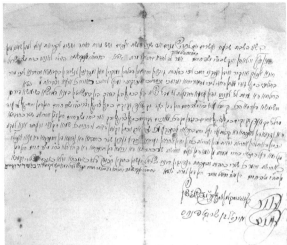

Below: This wedding portrait, which includes the families of the bride and groom, was taken in Bialystok in 1910.

The *shadkhen* (matchmaker) often acted as the final arbiter in this complicated system. Although anyone in the shtetl might promise, "Have I got a girl for you," the shadkhen made a profession of it. An ambitious marriage broker traveled from town to town keeping a careful watch on prospective candidates. He carefully weighed their qualifications trying to create the most desirable match for his clients. It was said that a truly gifted shadkhen could "bring two walls together."[31]

Undoubtedly some young people chafed at this outside intervention. And as increasing numbers of Jews moved to the city, they discovered a more flexible system of courtship based on modern ideals of romantic love and individual choice. Working among peers, girls found greater opportunities to meet men and more support to "follow their heart." But in the isolated world of the shtetl, old traditions held sway, and in struggles over authority it was the parents who usually emerged victorious. The circumstances of shtetl life depended on family solidarity, and children were raised to respect their parents. A son or daughter might resist a match, but open revolt was intolerable.

The collective values of the shtetl persisted in the face of extreme hardship. In contrast to the richness of a communal spiritual life, many Jews in these small communities lived a physical life of devastating poverty. When asked about food in the Old World, Rose Levine replied, "I got news for you—I think I was starving."[32] An immigrant from Kovno recalled that although her father was a cobbler, he could not afford shoes for his eight children. "My father was . . . as poor as he could be. . . . We wore bundles of straw tied fast to our legs with rags."[33] In the midst of such destitution, families struggled to survive. Sam Auspitz recalled that although his brother had a tailor shop and his mother worked as a seamstress in their small Czechoslovakian town, there was never enough food. "Just to stay alive," he said, was "the main object."[34]

inserting numerous tucks that could be released as the child grew.[37] An immigrant from Russia said that his family used to *ibernitzeven*, that is, turn the seams and wear the garment inside out, to prolong the life of old clothes.[38]

Maintaining the family's wardrobe was a labor-intensive task that Jewish women incorporated into their weekly routine. The lack of running water in a shtetl made washing even a meager supply of clothing an arduous chore. Writing for the *Boston Globe* in 1892, Frank Carpenter described a typical laundry day in a Russian peasant village:

> No Russian girl . . . ever sees a washboard nor has any ideas of washing machines or patent wringers . . . The clothes of the family are carried by her to the nearest stream, and standing in her bare legs in the water, she pounds the dirt out of them with a club.[39]

Bessie Cohen Akawie remembers accompanying her mother to the river to wash the clothing when she lived in Krasna: "We'd wash the [clothes] . . . with the hot water at home, and then rinse it at the river."[40] Similarly, an immigrant from White Russia recalls washing the clothes in a *zlitka* (a hollowed-out tree trunk) and then carrying the heavy load to the river for another soaping and a final rinsing. "After that we brought the clothes home to dry. Only special clothes were ironed, . . . but most of the clothes were rolled in a *ruber*, a piece of wood which looked like a rolling pin."[41] As Morris Cohen observed, the burden of laundering clothing and household textiles became even more onerous during the winter months when the river would freeze and "the washing had to be done through a hole in the ice."[42]

Delicate laces, fragile silks, and fussy trimmings had no place in the shtetl. Laboring Jewish women depended on durable fabrics and functional styles that covered the body without restriction. "No Russian peasant girl ever dreams of buying or wearing corsets or stays," wrote one contemporary observer. "Her outfit

Opposite above: A youth group in Poland. Young people sometimes resisted traditional arranged marriages, preferring the modern notion of marrying for love.

Opposite below: Economic conditions worsened for many Jews as government restrictions increased.

Above: Jewish women were a visible presence in Eastern European marketplaces.

Needs were reduced to the barest level of subsistence; luxuries such as stylish clothing were unheard of in the poorest shtetls. Struggling to keep their families warm and fed, parents clothed themselves and their children in layers of functional, not fashionable, garments. They often patched together outfits out of remnants. Nathan Gittleman recalled that when his family lived in Poland townspeople relied on the packages of shoes friends and relatives sent from America. People without this largesse walked around barefoot, wrapping rags around their feet in winter. Nathan's brother would bring home scraps of pelts from work. "We'd make our own shoes from the pelt," he said, "like . . . fur coat shoes."[35] Sara Rovner was not so fortunate. The money her father sent from America never arrived, and she and her family were constantly on the run trying to escape the pogroms so that they could come to the United States. "We were in cemeteries. We were sleeping in cellars. . . . I didn't have a pair of shoes until I was twelve."[36]

Clothing was a scarce and precious commodity, so garments were handed down from one child to the next, and mended many times. Mothers sewed oversized infant clothing,

. . . consists of this handkerchief for her head, [an ankle-length] Mother Hubbard gown of white cotton or red or blue calico . . . and an apron."[43] Women dressed simply in blouses, skirts, and aprons with layers of cotton or woolen petticoats worn underneath the skirt. Oversized woolen shawls were also a staple part of women's wardrobes. Durable and capacious, they ensured modesty by covering the shoulders and arms and provided warmth in the colder months.

Not all Jews lived in a constant climate of want. Many immigrants remember a life of relative comfort and pleasure. Esther Ginsburg's mother ran a dressmaking business in Lithuania. Her success enabled her to employ two servants to take care of the house and children, as well as five women who sewed for her. When asked about her homeland, Esther recalled "beautiful memories" filled with "roses—gardens smelling with roses."[44] Ida Ellis attributed her family's good fortune to her father's profession. "We lived very well because my father was . . . a scientist and as a result of that he had privileges more than the average person in Russia had."[45] The family was allowed to choose where they lived, and all of the seven children attended school.

Left: Caring for clothing could be an arduous task; these women wash clothes in a river. Above: Rebecca Rosenfield used this ruhlholtz, or washing tool, in Lithuania in about 1890.

The wool shawl was an essential part of a woman's wardrobe. Warm and functional, shawls often covered the wearer from head to toe. Jewish immigrants brought these shawls to the United States.

Prosperous Jews did not have to rely on secondhand goods and makeshift clothing; they purchased quality ready-made apparel or enlisted the services of a dressmaker. Minnie Laken lived in Russia until 1912 when, at the age of twelve, she emigrated to America. When asked if her mother sewed, Minnie replied, "No, she didn't. . . . We used to give away everything to a dressmaker." At each Passover celebration, there were "new dresses for the girls" and tailor-made "new suits for the boys."[46] Working as a dressmaker in Russia, Jennie Schaffner's mother studied Parisian fashion magazines. She would copy the styles for her clientele because "you go with the times."[47]

Regardless of their economic status, Orthodox women followed religious mandates of dress. It was not enough, however, for women to pattern their dress according to the principles of function or even tradition: the requirements of modesty, as defined by Jewish law, also had to be satisfied. The spirit of religious devotion that shaped the inner life of Eastern European Jews also defined critical aspects of a woman's appearance. Of primary importance was the covering of the head. In fulfillment of a *minhag* (custom), a married Jewish woman relinquished the privilege of wearing her hair uncovered.[48] After the wedding ceremony, an Orthodox woman would always appear in bonnets (*kupkes*), kerchiefs, or various forms of regional headdresses. Since hair was considered a woman's greatest ornament, this ritual was both an act of modesty and a public statement that the bride would hide her beauty from all men other than her husband.[49] The most observant women would shave their heads as part of the wedding preparations and put on a *sheitel* (wig).

For Ida Feldman, the sheitel fit into a simple equation. When asked about the customs of her home in Siedlac, Poland, she said, "In Europe you wear a wig. We were religious, you wear a wig."[50]

Many immigrants remember the sheitel as the most tangible barometer of the level of a woman's devoutness. A Polish woman from Warsaw made the distinction between her grandmother, a very religious woman who "wore a wig and observed all the customs," and her aunt who did not. Apparently, however, the aunt's rebellion had its limits. Whenever she visited her grandfather, who was a Chassid, "she wore a bang of artificial hair in front of her own hair."[61] Other women felt that the practice of wearing a sheitel was open to individual interpretation. Sophie Dobrin and Betty Feldman both described their mothers as religious, yet one woman kept her hair long and only wore a small sheitel to go to *shul* (synagogue) while the other resisted the teachings of her Orthodox rabbi father by refusing to ever put on a wig.[52] The self-conscious, and sometimes contradictory, choices women made underscore the conceptual richness of the clothing custom. Jewish women might struggle against the convention, modify it, maintain it, or reject it outright, but the tradition lived on as a measuring stick.

These patterns of dress were more style than fashion. Rather than changing a sleeve shape or hem length according to the season, Jewish women continued to adhere to a dress code that was centuries in the making. The basic style developed out of the regional European costumes that had been in existence since the seventeenth century. This fossilization of clothing, where change evolves so slowly that the style appears frozen in time, is characteristic of folk costume. Framed more by cultural values than fashionable fluctuations, recurring clothing styles link people to a shared sense of place, class, and experience.

Fashionable women knew the importance of accessories. This coin purse was worn draped over a finger.

Opposite: Illustrations from the Yiddish fashion magazine Die Mode, *which brought the latest styles to fashionable Jewish women in Warsaw.*

The bell-shaped skirt worn by this woman from Odessa was the fashionable silhouette at the turn of the century.

Left and opposite above:
Women wearing sheitels
in observance of Jewish
religious custom. In
1851 the Russian
government tried to
ban Jewish women
from wearing sheitels,
believing the practice
inhibited assimilation.

Rich in meaning, these clothing traditions served an essential function to the Jews. Constantly placed in the position of being outsiders, Jews continued to dress in a distinctive way that, in their eyes, defined them as insiders. Appearance functioned as a visual manifestation of ethnic identity and a self-conscious assertion of solidarity—a kind of cultural boundary marker. There is an old Jewish saying: "A custom is stronger than a law"; as symbol and strategy, clothing customs reflected deeply embedded values. Bound by a common fate and a shared heritage, the Jews of Eastern Europe held onto communal clothing traditions that became part of their tapestry of everyday life.

The Russian government understood the power of these symbols. Concluding that distinctive dress inhibited assimilation, they targeted Polish and Russian Jewish dress for extinction.[53] Beginning in the early nineteenth century, the government passed legislation designed to eliminate those aspects of appearance that qualified as distinctly Jewish. These laws forbade men to wear *peyes* (side locks) and banned women from wearing wigs. To encourage compliance, a sumptuary act of 1804 permitted greater travel privileges to Jews who adopted Russian dress.[54] Sterner measures were taken in 1848 when a tax was levied on yarmulkes. An 1851 Czarist decree focused upon the sheitel as one the most grievous offenses and ordered that:

> Jewish women must wear either ordinary caps or ladies' hats, dresses of ordinary cut similar to the ones worn by Russian women . . . It is forbidden to wear . . . false hair . . . Jewish women are to be inspected to discover whether or not they are shaving their heads; examination is to take place on the premises of local authorities in the presence of her husband or immediate relative.[55]

Right: Rifka Levinthal Perkins Hoffman, an Orthodox Jew from Russia, wore this sheitel, which is made of human hair.

That the Russian Council of State continued to issue these sumptuary laws reveals one important truth—the government had to keep passing legislation because Jews refused to conform. Eastern European Jews understood, with great clarity and wisdom, what clothing analysts have been struggling with for years. Ritual clothing is not just a cultural facade; it is a constant reminder of what is valuable and worthy.

Eastern European Jews judiciously used the acquisition of new garments to celebrate a special event. In this way, they translated cultural values into material form. Shmuel Rubenstein explains that the importance of this act is expressed in the Midrash (rabbinical commentaries on Biblical passages): "Bilam said to Bolok, how can I curse Israel when they honor the Sabbath and the Holidays with nice clothing."[56]

New garments were an essential part of Passover, the holiday that commemorates the deliverance of the Israelites from their captivity to the Egyptians. Women worked for weeks in preparation, cleaning the house from top to bottom, searching the corners and cupboards for any stray crumbs of leavened food, and readying the table for the Passover seders. The frenzy of activity surrounding these preparations is a lasting shtetl memory: everyone in the shtetl would wear their best outfits in celebration, and the anticipation of new clothing added greatly to the spirit of joy, purification, and rebirth. Stressing the importance of this aspect of the *Pesach* (Passover) tradition in a child's life, a woman who grew up in Bialystock recalled that "each child, even in the poorest family, gets something new to wear. . . And I believe that that is the only moment in the year when parents do not insist on buying clothes that are too large for the child by two or three sizes."[57]

This symbolic promise of something new also occurred at other holidays. A woman from Kovno remembered carrying a gift of *bub* (a bean) to her mother's wealthy relatives on Purim in the hopes of getting a special treat such as stockings or an *alte dresskele* (an old little dress). "I would run all the way home, yelling *'Mama! Ich hob'! Ich hob'!*" (Mama, I've got something!)[58]

Jews often acquired new clothing to celebrate the Sabbath or holidays. Geeta Schindler Rubenstein wore this dressy shawl in Russia in about 1885.

Below: In Pesach (Passover), Ilex Beller depicts the spirit of the prophet Elijah, who will announce the coming of the Messiah.

*Jews honor the Sabbath
and holidays with ritual
objects. The Kiddush
cups hold wine that
is consumed during
a prayer; candles are
lit to symbolize the
beginning of the
Sabbath or holiday;
and the decorative
cloth covers matzo,
the special unleavened
bread made for
Passover.*

Holiday luxuries such as an embroidered shawl, a silk bodice, or a velvet skirt would then be designated as Sabbath clothing. Many women reserved their *chuppah* (wedding) dress for this honor. A Russian immigrant, remembering the parade of women in their finery and men in their formal suits on their way to shul every Saturday, also recalled the creative solution his mother devised so that she, too, could appear her best on the Sabbath. In order to pay for his schooling, his mother had given the *melamud* (teacher) her pearls as a *mashkon* (pawn). "Every Friday night, the melamud brought my mother her pearls so that she could dress up to go to shul . . . and then, on Saturday night, mother would bring them back to him."[59]

Carefully stored apart from the weekday clothing in a separate closet or compartment, these treasured possessions fulfilled a crucial function. Keeping the Sabbath holy is one of the basic tenets of Jewish life. It is ushered in on Friday evening by the lighting of at least two candles representing the fourth commandment, to remember the Sabbath, and the twelfth verse in Deuteronomy to observe it.[60] From that moment until Saturday at sundown all forms of labor are forbidden. Lillian Levin remembered it as a family day. "On the Sabbath, we were detached from the outside world . . . and our house was our little kingdom." She also recalled her excitement as a young girl in Poland watching her mother put on her "shimmering" made-to-order silks, a gold watch and chain, and her special hats that were carefully packed away and taken out once a week. "It was a delight to watch mother prepare to go to the synagogue."[61] The ritual use of special objects consecrated this day, marking the end of the work week and signaling the importance of *Shabbos* as a time of celebration and spiritual renewal. Sarah Rothman's mother sorely felt the lack of a special Sabbath outfit. "My mother didn't have clothes to wear to Shul,"

This child's dress, lovingly embroidered by Sara Karp in Indura, Russia, probably made its debut on a holiday or the Sabbath.

Sarah remembered. "So she went on Rosh Hashanah and Yom Kippur only. And she used to feel very bad to come in an old coat."[62]

Amidst an atmosphere of deprivation and scarcity, this weekly demonstration of material splendor enabled the Jews to tangibly transform themselves and their world. This transformation symbolized the division between the spiritual and the mundane in the same way that the Sabbath table set with heirloom candlesticks and festive food marked the holiness of the day.[63] For Sally Gurian, living in a little town near Odessa, shoes signified a spiritual richness. "We ran around barefeet and the only time we had shoes on was Saturday, because that was a holy holiday."[64]

One of a Jewish woman's most important religious duties is to light the candles and say the blessing on the Sabbath. This pair of brass candlesticks belonged to Esther and Nathan Rushakoff, who lived in Ukraine.

Martin Buber told a story that eloquently explains the power of these rituals. It is a story of two men who question what makes the Sabbath holy. As a test, they celebrate the Sabbath in the middle of the week; alarmingly it works. The rituals of the Sabbath transcend the calendar. The men share their dilemma with the rabbi, who comments:

> If you put on Sabbath clothes and Sabbath caps it is quite right that you had a feeling of Sabbath holiness. Because Sabbath clothes and Sabbath caps have the power of drawing the light of the Sabbath holiness down to the earth. So you need have no fears.[65]

Although the shtetl community was certainly the most influential force in defining Eastern European Jewish culture, many Jews had moved away from small towns by the time of their immigration.[66] Larger Jewish settlements supported a variety of economic and cultural activities such as theater, newspapers, *gymnazia* (schools), and an active commerce district. Townspeople living in and around Knysyn, Poland, for instance, enjoyed the music of the town orchestra and string band.[67] Exposed to the social, cultural, and intellectual influences of the outside world, inhabitants witnessed the development of a modern consciousness in Eastern Europe. And just as the world that the immigrants would try to transplant was rooted in Eastern European soil, so too were the seeds of dissension.

The biblical injunctions and folk customs that thrived in the "island culture" of the shtetl now had to compete with the sophistication of more urban influences. Intellectual and political movements, such as the *Haskalah* (Jewish Enlightenment), that challenged traditional values found a receptive audience among Jewish youth.[68] Investigating the situation among Lithuanian Jews in 1898, the *Jewish Daily News* reported that "new thoughts have come to the younger generation. The monotonous whirr of

The city of Prague in the early twentieth century.

Left and opposite: Jewish youth groups such as these worked toward creating a modern, socialist society.

the winding spool, the rush of the webbing, are relieved by two ideas—Zionism, and the socialistic plea for an eight hours working day."[69]

Young people, growing impatient with their parents' conservatism, found in these radical movements persuasive grounds to argue for expanded rights. Their introduction to secular Western European culture also raised questions about Judaism itself. Not surprisingly, many parents found these challenges threatening. Raised in a conservative tradition built upon conformity and unquestioned authority, they strengthened their resolve to resist the forces of change. Fanny Shapiro's parents balked at the idea of Fanny leaving their small Russian town to go live in a city. "My people wouldn't let me go because socialism and many other progressive things were coming to life," she said. "My mother used to say to my father, 'She's liable to become a socialist and she'll drop the religion."[70] Mendel Sforim explored these conflicts in his book *Eltern Un Kinder* (*Parents and Children*). Published in Warsaw around 1910, the story describes the conflict between Efraim Karmol, a wealthy Orthodox man, and his children, Shimon and Rachel. Shimon, influenced by the Haskalah

philosophy, breaks away from the religious teachings of his father, while Rachel expresses her defiance by questioning her father's choice of a potential mate. Shimon encourages her rebellion, arguing that she, too, has rights. He asks, "Did you tell them with an open mouth the clear words that the parents do not have the right to do with their children whatever they want, to sell them and to marry them off without asking their opinion?" But ultimately, Rachel acquiesces because "she, like all Jewish girls, belongs with her heart and her soul to her father." Shimon, however, runs away to escape the same family pressures.[71]

This story illustrates more than a widening gulf between the generations; it also reinforces the nuances of individual experience. While some Jews wanted to cast off the relics of the Old World after their initiation into the heady world of urban life, others clung to familiar bonds of loyalty and obligation. And still other Jews struggled to find a balance between restraint and desire, between tradition and modernity.

The unfamiliar terrain of a city, which was itself in a state of flux, offered much to deal with, leaving neither the old nor the young unchanged. Removed from the "survival orientation" of rural villages, Jews discovered the possibility of choices, and a spirit of individualism invaded the consciousness of a people who for so long had struggled to preserve the community as a locus of power. New aspirations centered around the desirability of owning *things* questioned the pre-industrial model of consumption that was shaped by a spirit of religious devotion. In the shtetl, residents viewed any surplus food, money, or clothing as a gift to be shared with the community. Generosity brought great status within "a framework of mutual aid," and this value system survived the transatlantic crossing.[72] Whether through formal organizations such as the *landsmanshaftn*, immigrant benevolent societies, or informally through family and neighborhood ties, immigrant Jews united to provide social, economic, and cultural support to the new arrivals.

Yet the capitalist stirrings of the city introduced Jews to the sentiment of acquisitiveness. Here they developed an intimate knowledge of stylish refinements. Personal consumption did not replace benevolence, but it did offer an enticing layer of opportunity. Exposed to magazines, department stores, and the parade of urban abundance, more prosperous Jews could indulge their newly awakened desires. Some Jewish women avidly followed the fashion pronouncements from Paris, and it was more likely that they would follow fashion dictates rather than religious mandates. Living near Kiev, Lillian Kaiz's mother surrounded herself with fashionable statements of elegance. Lillian recalled their second-class voyage to America as a painful reminder of all that her family had left behind. "All my mother's jewels and furs were either taken or she sold them, and so when we got off the boat and we saw some women dressed beautifully I regretted that my mother didn't have her things any more."[73]

Cast in the reflection of city lights, the Orthodox world could seem archaic, provincial, and restrictive. Regardless of whether Jews continued to adhere to the tenets of a religious life or began to embrace a more secular view, it is certain that exposure to city life, however brief, eased their adjustment from Eastern Europe to the United States. Because even if they chose to resist the lure of consumption in the industrial centers of Russia and Poland, they would be tempted again once they reached American soil.

The crisis in Eastern Europe, however, overshadowed these opportunities. For most Jews, the promise of industrialization remained just that—a promise. Expelled from the cities in Russia's interior, Jews relocated to the cities in the Pale of Settlement, only to encounter a depressed economy with too few jobs and too

many workers.[74] Jews found themselves competing for jobs in a labor market already saturated with masses of Russian peasants who had migrated to the cities looking for work. Earning a livelihood proved more and more difficult.

Tragically, neither a change of residence, proletariat philosophies, nor political activism could protect them from the Czarist edicts that excised their freedoms. The Galician who looked at a passing train and dreamed that "somewhere else life is better, that the world is different, big, better, but not ours," had to look far beyond the Pale of Settlement for that better place.[75] Watching the traditional world of the shtetl erode and losing ground in the industrialized world because of rampant prejudice, Jews had to accept a fate of social vulnerability and political marginality.[76] Thus poverty was not the only reason Jews came to America; many came out of fear:

> So then there came the trouble and we had pogroms. . . . They used to rape girls, and my mother decided they should send me here. I didn't have a chance to get the passport and I went to the borderline stealing. . . . In those days, they were afraid for girls. Something might happen to them. It was dangerous just to be.[77]

A busy street in a Lithuanian city. Jews who lived in urban areas often had an easier time adjusting to life in America than their rural counterparts.

אבע רייך, א׳ן ארבייטער, 17 יאהר אלט, געטויטעט אויף דער דעמאָנסטראַציע אין דווינסק 4 מערץ ג. סט, 1905.
שלמה מאָרגאַלין, 22 יאָהר אלט, שווער פערוואונדעט אויף דער דעמאָנסטראַציע אין וואַרשאַו 2 אפריל ג. סט, געשטאָרבען דעם 5 אפריל 1905.
ע. כהן, געטויטעט אויף דער זעלבער דעמאָנסטראַציע.

This postcard commemorates the victims of the 1905 pogroms, which were sanctioned by the Russian government as a solution to the "Jewish problem."

Opposite: Russian soldiers lined up at a train station.

Punitive actions such as residence laws, travel limitations, occupational restrictions, and educational quotas were just part of an inexorable plan of persecution. More cruelly, the government sanctioned violent pogroms as a way to solve "the Jewish problem." Regardless of their economic status, Eastern European Jews faced escalating forms of discrimination as the government carried out a Draconian policy of extermination and expulsion. The following excerpt outlines part of the rationale behind the May Laws of 1881:

> The Government recognized that it is justified in adopting, without delay, no less energetic measures to remove the present abnormal relations that exist between the original inhabitants and the Jews, and to shield the Russian population against this harmful Jewish activity which, according to local information, was responsible for the disturbances.[78]

When immigrants speak of growing up within the shadow of this terrorism, the fear seems trapped in their memories. Sara Rovner recalled the "times when the soldiers would knock on your door and you wouldn't know what to say, whether to speak Polish or speak Russian, because they'll shoot you right through the door."[79] Gertrude Yellin's images of Bialystock are of "pogroms and hunger." "I don't even remember my being a child," she said.[80] And in her autobiography, *My Life*, Golda Meir presents a haunting portrait of a child's terror:

> I can remember how I stood on the stairs that led to the second floor, where another Jewish family lived, holding hands with their little daughter and watching our fathers trying to barricade the entrance with boards of wood. . . . To this day I remember how scared I was and how angry that all my father could do to protect me was to nail a few planks together while we waited for the hooligans to come. And, above all, I remember being aware that this was happening to me because I was Jewish.[81]

For millions of Jews, migration was no longer a choice—it was a necessity. By 1920, two million Jews remained in Eastern Europe, two million had perished from starvation, disease, and

*Immigrants on their
way to America in
Danzig, Germany,
with their baggage.
Faced with persecution
and poverty, two
million Jews left Eastern
Europe to find a better
life in America.*

violence, and two million had made their way to America.[82] But what were they coming to? To Golda Meir, the trip from Pinsk to America was "almost like going to the moon."[83] The letters sent from friends and family who had made the journey often presented a less than realistic picture of the life awaiting them. Sophia Kreitzberg imagined America as a place where "all the streets were paved with gold and you just picked up the gold and became rich and you sent for your family."[84] For Rose Levine, an eleven-year-old Russian girl, America was where a girl could have "wonderful things" such as dolls to play with and flying chairs carried people from place to place.[85] The reality of America would quickly dispel those inflated dreams, but the promise of opportunity and freedom helped sustain families through the long separations they endured and the difficulties they would have before them. And so family by family, Jews took a courageous

*Left: Immigrants
crowding the decks
of a ship. Below:
Candlesticks, feather
pillow, shawl, beads
and a clock. Forced
to pack up their past
in a trunk, immigrants
took their most valued
possessions.*

leap of faith, suffering the pain of leaving for the promise of a better life.

Determined to succeed in *di goldene medina* (the golden land), they looked toward the future; yet to understand the life they made in the New World, we must look back to di alte heym. For in addition to their trunks filled with pillows, samovars, candlesticks, and clothing, immigrants carried with them the values of their homeland where important lessons were learned: the enduring patterns of familial priorities; a community ethos steeped in religion, and the importance of rituals and clothing symbols that affirmed, as well as confirmed, a moral and social order. And it would be these lessons that connected them to their Jewishness and decisively shaped their response to the assimilation pressures that awaited them in America.

1. Fannie Friedman, Ellis Island Oral History Project, Ellis Island Immigration Museum.

2. Gilda Hochman, Ellis Island Oral History Project.

3. Lazarus Salamon, Ellis Island Oral History Project.

4. Barbara Myerhoff, *Number Our Days* (New York: 1978), 60–61.

5. Ruth Metzger, Ellis Island Oral History Project.

6. Mary Antin, *The Promised Land* (Boston: 1912), 1.

7. Irving Howe, *World of Our Fathers* (New York: 1983), 7.

8. Norma Fain Pratt, "Transitions in Judaism: The Jewish American Woman Through the 1930s," *American Quarterly* 30:5 (Winter 1978): 685.

9. Emanuel Kirwin, Ellis Island Oral History Project.

10. Vivian Mann, "Symbols of the Legacy: Family and Home," in David Altschuller, ed., *The Precious Legacy: Judaic Treasures from the Czechoslovak State Collections* (New York: 1983), 165.

11. Myerhoff, *Number Our Days*, 21.

12. Gerald Sorin, *A Time for Building: The Third Migration, 1880–1920* (Baltimore: 1992), 13.

13. Oscar Handlin, *The Uprooted: The Epic Story of the Great Migrations That Made the American People*, 2nd ed. (Boston: 1973), 12.

14. Margaret Mead Papers, Research in Contemporary Cultures, J-R 46, G45, Vol. 5, August 24, 1947, Library of Congress.

15. Bella Metz with Paul M. Levitt, "Diaspora," *Frontiers* 3:1: 68.

16. Antin, *The Promised Land*, 34.

17. Mina K. Friedman, Ellis Island Oral History Project.

18. Leslie Woodcock Tentler, *Wage-Earning Women: Industrial Work and Family Life in the United States 1900–1930* (New York: 1979), 16.

19. Susan A. Glenn, *Daughters of the Shtetl: Life and Labor in the Immigrant Generation* (Ithaca: 1990), 19–20.

20. Fannie Friedman, Ellis Island Oral History Project.

21. Myerhoff, *Number Our Days*, 233.

22. Antin, *The Promised Land*, 35.

23. N. F. Joffe, "The Family: Part III, Marriage," Margaret Mead Papers, Research in Contemporary Cultures, J-369, G49, vol. 17, September 1949.

24. Joffe, "The Family: Part III, Marriage."

25. Mark Zborowski and Elizabeth Herzog, *Life is With People: The Culture of the Shtetl* (New York: 1974), 136.

26. Dina Rosen, interview with author, February 12, 1993.

27. Margaret Mead Papers, Research in Contemporary Cultures, J-R 309, G46, vol. 11, April 1949.

28. Margaret Mead Papers, Research in Contemporary Cultures, J-P 343, G47, vol. 10, July 1949.

29. Morris Raphael Cohen, *A Dreamer's Journey* (reprint, New York: 1975), 112.

30. Sydney Stahl Weinberg, *The World of Our Mothers: The Lives of Jewish Immigrant Women* (Chapel Hill: 1988), 5.

31. Zborwoski and Herzog, *Life is with People*, 271.

32. Rose Levine, Ellis Island Oral History Project.

33. Margaret Mead Papers, Research in Contemporary Cultures, J-R 46, G45, vol. 5, August 24, 1947.

34. Sam Auspitz, Ellis Island Oral History Project.

35. Nathan Gittleman, Ellis Island Oral History Project.

36. Sara Milanow Rovner, Ellis Island Oral History Project.

37. Charlotte Baum, Paula Hyman, and Sonya Michel, *The Jewish Woman in America* (New York: 1975), 67.

38. Margaret Mead Papers, Research in Contemporary Cultures, J-R 36, G45, vol. 2, part 2, June 16, 1947.

39. Frank Carpenter, "100,000 Peasants," *Boston Sunday Globe*, August 21, 1892.

40. Bessie Cohen Akawie, Ellis Island Oral History Project.

41. Margaret Mead Papers, Research in Contemporary Cultures, J-R 32, G45, vol. 2, part 2, August 7, 1947.

42. Cohen, *A Dreamer's Journey* , 17–18.

43. Carpenter, "100,000 Peasants."

44. Neil Cowan and Ruth Schwartz Cowan, *Our Parent's Lives: The Americanization of Eastern European Jews* (New York: 1989), 16.

45. Ida Ellis, Ellis Island Oral History Project.

46. Minnie Laken, Ellis Island Oral History Project.

47. Jennie Schaffner, interview with Eden Rosenbush, June 19, 1993.

48. Rev. Dr. Wolff, Universal-Agende fur Kultusbeamte (Berlin: 1891) quoted in Rabbi L. Weiss, "The Jewess at Home and Abroad," *American Jewess* 1 (June 1895): 114–15.

49. Zborowski and Herzog, *Life is With People*, 271.

50. Ida Feldman, Ellis Island Oral History Project.

51. Margaret Mead Papers, Research in Contemporary Cultures, J-P 27, G45, vol. 3, July 28, 1947.

52. Sophie Dobrin, interview with Eden Rosenbush, May 29, 1993.

53. Alfred Rubens, *A History of Jewish Costume* (New York: 1973), 11.

54. *The Jewish Encyclopedia*, vol. IV (New York: 1903), 302.

55. Ludmila Uritskaya, "Ashkenazi Jewish Collections from the State Ethnographic Museum in St. Petersburg" in *Tracing An-sky: Jewish Collections from the State Ethnographic Museum in St. Petersburg* (Zvolle: 1992), 44.

56. Shmuel Rubenstein, *The Appearance of the Jew* (New York: 1973), 11.

57. Margaret Mead Papers, Research in Contemporary Cultures, J-P 132, G46, vol. 6-A, January 3, 1948.

58. Margaret Mead Papers, Research in Contemporary Cultures, J-R 46, G45, vol. 5, August 19, 1947.

59. Margaret Mead Papers, Research in Contemporary Cultures, J-R 32, G45, vol. 2, part 2, August 19, 1947.

60. Lis Harris, *Holy Days: The World of a Hasidic Family* (New York: 1985), 62.

61. Lillian Keidan Levin, "Transitions: Bringing Jewishness from Poland to America—My Mother's Reminiscences and Stories," unpublished manuscript, 1993, courtesy of Judith Levin Cantor.

62. Sorin, *A Time for Building*, 13.

63. Andrew Heinze, *Adapting to Abundance: Jewish Immigrants, Mass Consumption, and the Search for American Identity* (New York: 1990), 53–56.

64. Sally Gurian, Ellis Island Oral History Project.

65. Myerhoff, *Number Our Days*, 105.

66. Cowan and Cowan, *Our Parents' Lives*, 5.

67. Michael R. Weisser, *A Brotherhood of Memory: Jewish Landsmanshaftn in the New World* (Ithaca: 1985), 56.

68. Lucjan Dobroszycki and Barbara Kirshenblatt-Gimblett, *Image Before My Eyes: A Photographic History of Jewish Life in Poland, 1864–1939* (New York: 1977), 155.

69. "Russian Poland As It Is Today Among the Lithuanian Jews," *Jewish Daily News*, May 30, 1898.

70. Fanny Shapiro, Ellis Island Oral History Project.

71. Mendel Moche Sforim, *Eltern Un Kinder* (Warsaw: c. 1910) quoted in Mark Zborowski, "Eastern European Jewry: Parent-Child Relationships," Margaret Mead Papers, Research in Contemporary Cultures, J-131, G46, vol. 8.

72. Elizabeth Ewen, *Immigrant Women in the Land of Dollars: Life and Culture on the Lower East Side, 1890–1925* (New York: 1985), 46–47.

73. Lillian Kaiz, Ellis Island Oral History Project. 7

75. Eva Morawski, "For Bread with Butter: Life Worlds of Peasant Immigrants from East Central Europe, 1880–1914," *Journal of Social History*, Spring 1984: 389.

76. Glenn, *Daughters of the Shtetl*, 31–32.

77. Cowan and Cowan, *Our Parents' Lives*, 37.

78. Simon Dubnow, *History of the Jews in Russia and Poland*, vol. II (Philadelphia: 1920), 271.

79. Sara Rovner, Ellis Island Oral History Project.

80. Gertrude Yellin, Ellis Island Oral History Project.

81. Golda Meir, *My Life* (New York: 1975) reprinted in Maxine Schwartz Seller, ed., *Immigrant Women* (Philadelphia: 1981), 37.

82. Moses Rischin, *The Promised City: New York's Jews, 1870–1914* (Cambridge: 1962), 20.

83. Ivan Chermayeff, Fred Wasserman, and Mary J. Shapiro, *Ellis Island: An Illustrated History of the Immigrant Experience* (New York: 1991), 26.

84. Sophia Kreitzberg, Ellis Island Oral History Project.

85. Rose Levine, Ellis Island Oral History Project.

Traffic jam on Chicago's Dearborn Street looking south from Randolph Street, 1909. Immigrants, especially those from rural areas, discovered a bustling and often confusing world upon their arrival in America.

They Don't Wear Wigs Here

They don't wear wigs here." These were Yekl's words of greeting to his wife, Gitl, upon her arrival in America in Abraham Cahan's story, *Yekl, A Tale of the New York Ghetto*. At the end of her long journey from Russia, Gitl puts on the sheitel not only to honor the Sabbath but to celebrate the long-awaited reunion with Yekl. The symbolism, however, is lost on her Americanized husband. During their three-year separation, he has frantically embraced the customs of his new home, changing his name to Jake and rejecting his religious heritage. The image of his bewigged wife is a painful reminder of the past he is trying to forget. From the moment that Gitl steps off the boat at Ellis Island, Jake begins his relentless criticism of her dowdy appearance. Much of his anger is directed towards Gitl's "voluminous wig of a pitch-black hue." Rejecting her protestations that she wanted to spruce "herself up for the big event," Jake flatly informs her, "They don't wear wigs here."[1] Gitl reluctantly exchanges her sheitel for a scarf; unfortunately, this also fails to meet Jake's expectations of an Americanized wife, who would naturally sport a fashionable hat. As Gitl struggles to reconcile her husband's injunctions with her religious convictions, her appearance becomes both an expression and an extension of her painful adjustment to America.

Cahan's fictional account of clothing as an outward manifestation of a character's changing social and cultural consciousness closely mirrors the experiences of many immigrant women. Recounting her arrival at Ellis Island in 1921, Ida Feldman tells the story of a fellow passenger for whom the wig played a pivotal role. Before coming to America, she received a letter from her husband cautioning her to let her hair grow because "in America you don't wear no wigs." Unfortunately, the woman contracted typhoid fever while in Poland and lost her hair; thus, she wore her sheitel on the passage over to cover her bald head. When her husband spotted her, he concluded by her appearance that she was unwilling to make the necessary sartorial adjustments, and he angrily refused to take her off of the island. Townspeople found a home for the woman and her three children; eventually she reconciled with her husband, but "she wore a wig the rest of her life."[2]

To newly arrived immigrants a change of clothes was the most visible way they could identify themselves as American Jews. This first act of initiation helped to blur the obvious differences between the "greenhorn" and the "real" Americans; it also offered tangible proof that the cultural chasm confronting the newcomers could be bridged. Learning the language would prove the ultimate test of assimilation, but mastering English often took years of study. How much easier it was to embrace the symbolic language of American clothing. It is no wonder that "great stress [was] placed upon clothes."[3] Immigrants exchanged the garments of the Old World for the fashions of the New World with the passion of individuals intent on self-transformation.

While all urban immigrants recognized clothing as the important first step of assimilation, Jewish immigrants embraced the concept with extraordinary zeal. Unlike other new émigrés who came to America with the intention of returning to the homeland, the vast majority of Jews envisioned their move as permanent. As the situation in Eastern Europe declined, Jews feared not just for their livelihoods but for their

Above and opposite left and right: The decision to wear a wig, kerchief, or hat was often a defining one for new immigrants.

safety. Faced with the realities of political oppression, anti-Semitic Czarist restrictions, and worsening economic conditions, Jews escaped to America determined to make a new life for themselves in *di goldene medina*. Recounting his early experiences as an immigrant from the Ukraine, Dr. Morris Moel

In the Land of the Free, rapid changes we see.

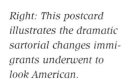

Right: This postcard illustrates the dramatic sartorial changes immigrants underwent to look American.

explained that coming to America "was something that you longed for and . . . even though we came under difficulties and it was somewhat difficult to adjust . . . it was the greatest land that we could imagine."[4]

The settlement pattern of Jewish immigrants also contributed to their rapid adoption of American styles. The suffering of Jews in Eastern Europe affected all socioeconomic classes, and the émigrés represented every rung in the social ladder. While much has been written about the impoverishment of the shtetl dwellers, the story must also include the Eastern European Jews who enjoyed relative prosperity. In contrast to the staggering poverty of the many Jewish peasants, other Jews earned an income much higher than the subsistence level.[5] Many lived in burgeoning industrial centers where they were exposed to new political, secular, and cultural ideas, as well as the broader world of consumption. Gill Sherrid's family enjoyed great prestige in their Russian community. His mother used to tell him about her clothing: "Everything was made to order and she was the most beautifully dressed young woman in town."[6] Gill's mother was not alone. Among the vast numbers of Jews who arrived in America between 1880 and 1920, a percentage of them came with a decidedly modern orientation.

Furthermore, nearly half of the Jewish emigrants were female, and many of them were unmarried women in their teens and twenties. Only the Irish sent a greater proportion of women to America.[7] Young Jewish women brought with them a unique set of values and concerns that was shaped as much by their Eastern European heritage as by their hopes for the future. Raised in an economy that depended upon female labor, many Jewish women came armed with experience as dressmakers or seamstresses. Willing to work, longing for an education, and aspiring to greater prosperity, this transitional generation of émigrés had the personal resources and vocational skills required to adapt to their new and strange surroundings. Certainly all newcomers had to confront the unfamiliar and deal with the pangs of separation, but youth had the advantage. Rather than struggling to transplant all of the customs of the Old Country, they willingly sought out the opportunities awaiting them. As active participants in the assimilation

Left and opposite: Many Eastern European Jewish immigrants came from relative prosperity and brought with them a familiarity with the modern world of consumption.

Dora Maremont Wolfson, left, came from a rural area of Eastern Europe in about 1880. She quickly embraced the fashionable American styles of a shirtwaist, tailored skirt, and pompadour hairstyle.

Opposite: Some
immigrants had
difficulty understanding
urban American ways.
Estelle Belford's mother
came from a poverty-
stricken shtetl in 1905.
When she saw clothes-
lines stretched between
buildings, she concluded
that Americans must
have very tall ladders
to be able to hang their
wash so high.

process, youth developed their own ethnic culture, drawing upon the past for support but eager to take on an expanded role.

David Blaustein, superintendent of New York's Educational Alliance, a settlement program established to assist newly arrived Jewish immigrants with domestic and vocational skills, wrote in 1902 that "there is no greater change from Eastern Europe to America than the change in the life of women."[8] Adjusting to the New World meant coming to terms with poverty, loneliness, and alienation. But for older women it also meant dealing with the daily demands of family life and running a household while coping with strange customs that often seemed incomprehensible. When Estelle Belford's mother left her impoverished shtetl in Romania to come to America in 1905, she could not begin to grasp all of the differences. The first time she looked out of her tenement window and saw the lines of washed clothing stretched from building to building, she asked her husband, "In America they have such big ladders that they climb up to hang the wash?"[9] Social worker Sophonisba Breckenridge noted in her 1921 study of immigrant women in Chicago that, because of the constantly changing standards in America, an immigrant woman "must learn to do things in a way her mother never dreamed of doing them."[10]   .

The urban areas where most Jews settled were lively, crowded, concrete environments that magnified sights, sounds, and smells. Although most immigrants settled in ghetto neighborhoods among other Eastern European Jews and therefore found familiar faces, language, and customs, the larger world continued to encroach upon these "centers of ethnic intensity."[11] Anna Kuthan remarked that the strangeness of her new home demanded her constant attention. "There was so many things that you can't figure out when you land here."[12] Jews who came from urban areas in Eastern Europe

undoubtedly had an easier time. When asked if she found America overwhelming Rose Jaffee replied that she had little trouble adjusting because she'd "seen it all before in St. Petersburg."[13] Yet while Rose remained undaunted by her first encounters with America, women from small impoverished shtetls looked at their new home with bewilderment.

Struggling with the transition, women tried to reconcile their visions of America with the stark reality of ghetto life. Home was typically a dark tenement apartment that offered only cold running water and a toilet at the end of the hall. Struggling to make ends meet, extended families crowded into two or three rooms, and women still had to take in piecework and boarders to eke out a living. For Sonia F., the garbage, noise, and crowds were painful contrasts to the "trees and cleanliness" she left behind in Kiev. Overwhelmed by homesickness, Sonia did not understand why her family had come "since it was so terrible" in the United States.[14] Back in Eastern Europe, Jews dreamed of a land of opportunity where "it would be gold in the streets, laying waiting for you."[15] Instead they found themselves in congested surroundings characterized by poverty and privation. After coming to America, Mina Friedman's mother spent her days struggling with domestic responsibilities while her husband worked sixteen hours a day in a sweatshop. The exhausting demands of "shopping from one pushcart to another, dragging up the food six flights of stairs, washing clothes in a steaming boiler," and caring for four children left little time to enjoy America's pleasures.[16]

Poverty was a particularly bitter reality to accept for those women who had left behind a life of comfort. Sara Abrams recalled that during her family's "period of reconciliation" with America, amid the conflicting emotions of peace, anger, and contentment, "a strain of sadness seemed to permeate our surroundings." The family's constant struggle for money contrasted sharply with the prosperity they had enjoyed in Poland. Sara remembered that her mother's friends would see her at the sewing machine and lament:

> The *goldene medina*. They used to tell us America was full of honey. They used to say, they shovel gold on the streets, and a woman like us, has to sit and sew, like a serving woman.[17]

Jewish women who escaped the destitution of their old home only to find themselves in another impoverished situation also felt acute frustration. Their disappointment, however, was mediated by America's promise that poverty did not have to be a life sentence. The tangible symbols of upward mobility pierced through their suffering as a talisman of the American dream. Deeply impressed by America's offering, Jews quickly developed an appetite for a new standard of living. The lyrics of "Men Shart Gold in America" pokes fun at such aspirations, but the words contain an important truth. In the song, Abie's wife agrees to follow him to America, but her acquiescence comes with strings attached. "Silks and satins I must vear ev'ry night in te-ay-ters and roast duck chickens every day no more 'herring mit potatoes' and to all dis Abie let me tell dot I must have a 'Merry Vidow' Hat." Through their acquisition of American products Jewish immigrants communicated their desire to fit into their new home; to be American, they had to look American.

Immigrants intent upon refashioning themselves did not lack for advice. Oral histories are filled with accounts of relatives who had already emigrated to this country schooling the newly arrived immigrants on the finer points of dressing. Sophie Abrams remembered going shopping with her aunt on her first day in America:

> She bought me a shirtwaist . . . and a skirt, a blue print with red buttons and a hat, such a hat I had never seen. I took my old brown dress and shawl and threw them away! I know it sounds foolish, we being so poor, but I didn't care. . . . When I looked in the mirror . . . I said, boy, Sophie, look at you now. . . just like an American.[18]

For the majority of Eastern European Jewish women, hairstyles and head coverings were the first crucial tests of looking American. The Orthodox law that required married women to cut off their hair and don a sheitel clashed with the fashionable American ideal. In the words of a fashion editor in 1905, a heavy head of hair was a woman's "crown of blessing."[19] The cult of bobbed hair belonged to the next generation of women; turn-of-the-century trendsetters took great pride in their long, luxuriant hair piled high into massive pompadours. Enormously important in the definition of female beauty, hair also carried a potent sexuality.[20] Thus, women captured their siren-like tresses into artfully arranged coiffures as a badge of maturity and respectability. The celebrated

Above: Illustrations from the November 1909 issue of The American Magazine, *which contained an article about the elaborate hairstyles favored by American women. The most intricate styles required hairpieces such as rats, fringes, switches, and braids (below).*

Above right: Many women resisted forsaking their traditional head-coverings for more fashionable hairstyles. Below: Sarah Karp brought this cotton print kerchief to the United States from Russia in 1906.

innocence of young girls enabled them to wear their hair down and often caught at the nape of the neck with an oversized stiffened bow. For Russian immigrant Fanny Gilbert, the fashion rule was absolute. "Oh my God," she recalled, "how could you go without a bow?"[21]

As a result of America's fascination with hair, the frankly artificial appearance of the coarse, stiffened wig created a clear line of demarcation between the religious old and the secular new. In his 1909 portrait of New York's Lower East Side, writer Hutchins Hapgood characterized the "Orthodox Jewess" as a drab woman, "plain in appearance, with a thick waist [and] a wig."[22] This image contrasted sharply with the "up-to-date" shopgirls whose feather-trimmed hats perched precariously on top of their fashionable hairstyles. These popular upswept styles required long, thick hair that could be twisted and securely pinned on top of the head. For those women with less-than-voluminous tresses, artificial hairpieces known as "rats" helped create the proper illusion.

After studying Jewish immigrant girls in Chicago in 1913, Viola Paradise concluded that "almost immediately upon the girl's arrival her relatives buy for her American clothes, usually a suit, a large hat, and not infrequently, the wherewithal to fix her hair in an American fashion." Paradise went on to quote one new-comer who proudly announced: "Yes, I'm

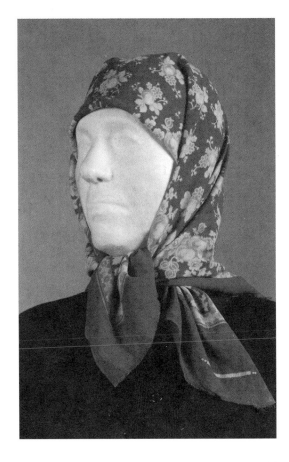

Vol. I. No. 2.

The Jewish Ladies Home Journal

May, 1913.

די פרויען וועלט

א מאנאטשריפֿט געװידמעט די אינטערעסען פֿון דער אידישער פֿרוי און דער אידישער היים.

רעדאקטירט פֿון א. גרייזעל

SHULAMITE   שולמית

די געליעבטע פֿון דעם קעניג שלמה ערװאַכט פֿון איהר דרעמיל און הערט זיך צו
בײם ענטציהונג צו דער הײסער ליעבעס-ליעד װאָס טראָגט זיך פֿון נאַרטען.

סובסקריפֿשאָן פרייז : 50 פ. יעהרליך, 25 פ. האלב יעהרליך

THE HEBREW EDUCATIONAL PUBLISHING COMPANY, 65-67 SUFFOLK STREET, NEW YORK, N. Y.

Opposite: Bessie Adler (standing) and her friends pose at Chicago's Riverview Park in their oversized hats. Above: Di Froyen-Velt advised Jewish women on fashion.

almost like an American. I have a rat for my hair."[23] Interestingly, in 1913 *Di Froyen-Velt* (the Jewish *Ladies' Home Journal*) used the growing prejudice against the sheitel to try to convince women to resist the fashionable use of hairpieces. Attacking the current trend in rats as blatantly artificial, the editors reminded readers of the hard-won battle to abolish the "old-fashioned" wigs that "our grandmothers and in part our mothers wore" with their "pious God-fearing expressions." They insisted

that "only those with no sense for beauty can afford to pull on their heads a piece of dead animal that disgusts anyone with a sense of aesthetics."[24]

Although many women discarded their wigs as a sign of American freedom, their more traditional counterparts perceived this act as a "concession to American godlessness."[25] This certainly was the case with an elderly woman who arrived at Ellis Island in 1902. Rejecting the newly purchased hat offered by her waiting relatives, she declared, "I am only an old-fashioned Jewess and I won't part with my wig. It's rather late to begin sinning."[26] Her family relented, probably because of her age. Ida Ellis's relatives were not so easily deterred. After their first week in America, Ida's parents invited family members to visit their new apartment. One of the cousins ("the Americanized one") came in, walked over to Ida's mother, and, without warning, pulled off her wig. "My mother said, 'Oh, my God! What are you doing to me?!'" to which the cousin replied, "In America you're not going to wear a wig."[27]

Discarding the wig was just the beginning of the immigrants' visual metamorphoses. Most Eastern European women arrived at Ellis Island wearing a kerchief as part of their native costume. While more elaborate headdresses might be worn on holidays and festive occasions, the simple scarf had survived intact as part of an Orthodox Jew's costume from its beginnings in the eighteenth century.[28] Although this traditional head covering was considered an integral part of a woman's *Yiddishkeit* (Jewishness), the immigrants quickly learned that in America decorative hats were more than an accessory; they were an essential component of the feminine toilette. Turn-of-the-century hats were impressive concoctions, and a lady never appeared in public without one.

Women changed their hats to suit the occasion, the time of day, and their moods. The straw boater worn with tailored skirts and simple cotton blouses would hardly have flattered an afternoon suit or a showy evening dress. The well-stocked feminine closet contained a great variety of millinery designs, each properly stored in its own hatbox. For the new arrivals, hats became a sensitive barometer of one's fashion sense, because hat styles changed with each season. Reporting on the proliferation of millinery stores on the Lower East Side in 1900, the *New York Tribune* noted that Division Street was home to at least twenty hat shops. Sacrificing quality for quantity, these stores devised creations that met the working girl's pocketbook and her craving for a flashy accessory. Reporting that "purple and yellow is a favorite combination" because of its dramatic effect, the paper described the average East Side girl's winter hat as large and sometimes groaning "beneath the weight of nearly or quite a dozen plumes."[29]

These confections of silk, feathers, and straw evoked more than stylishness; they became a symbol of American respectability and social aspirations. When Shaya, the Russian Talmudic scholar in Abraham Cahan's story *The Imported Bridegroom*, first sees a photograph of his intended bride, he is awed by her hat. Surely this woman "in all her splendor of Grand Street millinery" must be a princess.[30] His confusion is understandable in light of prevailing customs. In some parts of Eastern Europe only women of high social status could wear hats; therefore, wearing the latest millinery fashion meant "stepping out of the serving class, and out of the ranks of the peasants."[31] For Masha, in Anzia Yezierska's autobiographical novel *Bread Givers*, it only took ten-cents worth of pink paper roses purchased from a pushcart on Hester Street to make her feel "like a lady from Fifth Avenue."[32] A fashion-conscious woman featured in a Yiddish cartoon transformed her outdated hat into an up-to-the-minute pancake style by stomping on it. Delighted with the results, she

exclaimed: "Oh, my dears! How that hat suits me! My neighbor will burst with envy when she sees this special hat!"[33]

Paper roses, a scrap of ribbon, and several strategically placed feathers could turn a simple straw hat into a masterpiece. But not every young girl was satisfied with a homemade model. In her book *The House on Henry Street*, settlement-house worker Lillian Wald describes her role as arbiter in a family dispute over a hat. The mother came to Wald complaining about her daughter's extravagant purchase of a twenty-five-dollar hat with a "marvelous" feather plume. The mother, reassured that the

While venting her frustration, this woman discovers an unexpected solution to her fashion dilemma.

Above: Women changed hats to suit the occasion, time of day, and even their moods.

Right: Becoming American meant accepting a new body type. This stylish woman wore a tightly laced corset to create a wasp-waisted figure, the fashionable— if unnatural— ideal at the turn of the century.

money came from her daughter's overtime wages, agreed to refrain from nagging. The young girl, in turn, confessed her embarrassment over such extravagance. The pure pleasure of spending, however, remained undiminished: "It had been an orgy," she said.[34]

When twelve-year-old Celia Adler arrived in America in 1914, she discovered that it was not enough just to wear a hat; you had to wear the right kind of hat. Traveling alone from Russia to meet her sister, she proudly wore the sailor hat given to her by a friend as a going-away present. For Celia, this hat, the first she had ever owned, "was my whole treasure." But her sister identified the old-fashioned style as the badge of a greenhorn and insisted that Celia leave the hat behind on the dock at Ellis Island. "She was sure that anyone who will see me will know that I just got off the boat. And she didn't want it."[35]

Discarding the sheitel and replacing the kerchief with a wide-brimmed hat was just the first of many steps. Immigrant women spoke longingly of elegant American shoes with thin soles and high heels. While the everyday laced or buttoned boots were rarely ornamented, more dressy shoes featured thin kid leather, curved heels, and decorative bows or buckles. And well-to-do ladies encased their legs in color-coordinated, thin silk stockings. By contrast, the thick soles and sturdy laces of their Old World boots worn with heavy woolen stockings made the immigrants' feet appear huge, clumsy, and hopelessly out of style. Rose Cohen's aunt agreed. She bought Rose a "very pretty pair of black patent-leather slippers" for her to wear when she arrived on American soil because "shoes more than any other article of clothing showed the greenhorn."[36]

Sixteen-year-old Elizabeth Repshis's footwear immediately marked her as a foreigner. She arrived in 1913 wearing a pink blouse and skirt made for her by a dressmaker in Lithuania. Wishing to save her father any further expense, however, she wore her old patched shoes that each weighed "maybe about three pounds." In Elizabeth's eyes, this was the critical clothing message. "I looked foreign . . . with these big shoes," she said.[37] In her 1921 study of Chicago immigrants, Sophonisba Breckenridge concluded that shoes were one of the most volatile points of contention between the generations. While girls were drawn to the costly high-heeled fashion, mothers argued in favor of sensible, durable shoes that could be bought "at less than half the price."[38]

Reporting on fads in 1898, the *Jewish Daily News* noted that Jewish girls "generally have a weakness for a No. 3 shoe and although they

For many women the corset was uniquely American.

have a [big] Chicago foot they wear shoes as near the fashionable number as possible."[39] Trade journals also commented on the rapid adoption of shoe styles among immigrants. The *Shoe Retailer*, for example, claimed that "Americanizing usually starts at the foot, and except with those who are too old to heed the changes of the times, the familiar homemade footwear soon succeeds the more picturesque fashion of the new world."[40]

The contrast between the Old and New World styles was particularly striking for those newcomers who grew up in the poorer shtetls of Eastern Europe. When ten-year-old Fannie Shoock arrived at Ellis Island in 1921 and spied her first pair of American shoes, she thought that New Yorkers must have something wrong with their feet. After years of going barefoot or wearing hand-me-down shoes and wrapping woolen strips around her feet when the hand-me-downs wore out, how else could she explain these high-buttoned shoes with their

Right: Jewish vendors selling shoes on New York's Lower East Side. Below left: Zelda Asch Merewitz purchased these fashionable lace-up boots on the Lower East Side in 1918. Lower right: Early twentieth-century shoes.

exaggerated pointy toes? "I never saw high-top shoes before, but the toes are pointy like . . . the foot only had one toe. And I was thinking to myself, my God, what's wrong here, what . . . kind of country is this? People have pointy feet."[41]

The corset also figures prominently in the acculturation process because embracing the American ideal meant accepting a new body type. When Rose R. arrived from Bialystok in 1907, she discovered that her figure was in vogue. Stylish women had "big busts, big behinds and small waistlines. And I was just built like that."[42] Union organizer Rose Schneiderman recalled the despair she felt standing in front of a mirror with a critical eye. At ninety pounds, she could boast neither the bosom nor the "good-sized hips" of the American Gibson girl. A corset solved part of her problem; she discovered that "if you wore a short corset and laced it tight, your hips stuck out." To her dismay, improving her bosom proved more difficult.[43]

Most women, however, suffered from the opposite problem: being overweight by American standards. While the fullness of the fashionable turn-of-the-century silhouette could hardly be classified as willowy, the ideal shape, with its carefully defined curves, was conspicuously molded into unnatural proportions. The solid frame of many Eastern European women was too unmanaged for popular taste. Without the contrast of a small waist, a woman with full breasts and solid hips appeared large rather than curvaceous, and she could be ridiculed for her "Jewish figure."[44] Despite one mother's proud claim that, in her youth, her "shape was something to look on—not the straight up and down like the beauties make themselves in America," many women tried to emulate the American ideal with its leaner, svelte body.[45] They quickly realized that the fashionable wasp-waisted figure was possible only with the aid of a tightly laced corset.

Above: Many Eastern European women, like the Levinthal sisters, had naturally full figures. Such women needed a corset (left) to achieve the small waist that fashion demanded.

While numerous well-to-do women in Eastern Europe had already come to depend on the molded shaping and armored support of corsetry, for poorer women who lived in remote villages, the corset was uniquely American. Gertrude Yellin recalled her mother traveling to the Bronx to visit her eldest daughter.

Like many women's magazines, Di Froyen-Velt *offered its readers mail-order patterns and instructions.*

At the end of her one-year stay, she returned to Bialystock, Russia, a different person:

> She came to the United States as a plain, ordinary, poorly. . . . dressed woman, but came home as a lady. . . . She brought a whole trunk of clothes. And all our neighbors and all the family came to see the miracle of my mother's coming home. She even wore a corset. Why, in those years who would know?[46]

Endless opportunities seemed to await the Jewish woman intent upon becoming American. As the most tangible proof of assimilation, a new set of clothes could almost magically transform a newcomer's status from poverty to prosperity. It also reinforced a deeply rooted desire among Jewish immigrants to be accepted in their new homeland.[47] Later, the realization that Americans embraced their own code of social ranking would set in along with the knowledge that cultural adaptation went far beyond material possessions and external symbols. But in the first flush of excitement, the newcomers envisioned a world of unlimited possibilities (if not for themselves, at least for their children). Even though the multilayered rules governing the intricacies of American style and status continued to be set by the outside society, the symbolic relationship between clothing and identity was widely understood within the immigrant community.

While the delicate fabrics, expensive trimmings, and intricate construction of the most expensive clothes were beyond the means of most new arrivals, resourceful women became adept at recycling, remodeling, and assembling fashionable outfits from precious little. Yiddish newspapers and journals contained sewing instructions and patterns of styles that were "very easy to make." Every issue of *Di Froyen-Velt* , for example, included descriptions of four to six styles. Many of the patterns, which could be ordered directly from the magazine, featured several variations; semiprincess gown #7863 could be made in two neckline styles with short or long sleeves.[48] When advising women on summer dressing in 1898, the *Jewish Daily News* explained that for those clever enough to make their dresses, an extensive wardrobe could be had for only a few dollars.[49]

Women scoured the neighborhood for bargains, purchasing material from pushcart vendors, frequenting secondhand shops, and bringing home scraps from the cutting-room floor that could later be fashioned into "American" clothing. Their goal was style, not durability. Stylish clothing became especially important for young, unmarried women. Within the domestic family circle, purchasing a piano, upholstered furniture, or a sewing machine was often the critical initiation rite of consumption, but for young girls, new clothing was the first priority. "The working girl's clothes are her background, and from them she is largely judged," wrote Jane Addams.[50]

In one remarkable case, a working girl discovered the importance and the consequences of this judgment. Her potential employers read far more into the girl's outfit than her fashion sense: they interpreted her clothing as a political statement. While living in Russia, this young Jewish girl clothed herself in dresses "made out of sack, old sheets, or table cloths." Noticing the leather jackets worn by students and activists during the 1905 Revolution, she seized on this style as a "symbol both of Revolution and elegance." Her admiration for the jacket survived the transatlantic crossing, and it was one of her first purchases in America. In her long and fruitless search for permanent employment, one supervisor explained that they would not hire her because they did not like Bolsheviks, pointing to the girl's jacket and "bushy hair" as proof of her Communist leanings. After a year of frustration, she decided to get rid of the jacket:

> I dressed myself in the latest fashion, with lipstick in addition, although it was so hard to use at first that I blushed, felt foolish, and thought myself vulgar. But I got a job.[51]

Most working girls, however, had no interest in preserving the styles left behind in Eastern Europe. Far more interested in "greening themselves out," they became avid students of American fashion. Unlike many of their mothers who stayed within the safe enclave of the neighborhood, young working women explored the broader reaches of urban life. Consequently, they cultivated a sharp awareness of the dress and social mores of urban Americans. Contemporary observers frequently commented on the stylishness of young immigrant women, singling out the urban Jewish girl who worked in the factory or in the shop as a trendsetter among her peers. After visiting the home of a Jewish department-store clerk in 1903, one reporter noted the girl's elevated position, not only in her family but in her neighborhood as well: "Bessie . . . was the queen—for she was a saleslady! She dictated fashion to the whole tenement house and everybody in it imitated her and envied her."[52]

In the eyes of others, however, the "daughters of Israel" carried their love of finery to dangerous extremes. Both the Yiddish and English press criticized the new arrivals' penchant for overdressing. In December 1900 the *Jewish Daily News* asked why young girls could not "lay aside their traditional love for gewgaws and vulgar finery and instead of spending their time in devising how they may add another feather to their attire, learn to dress quietly and tastefully?"[53] Later that month the paper ran another article accusing young girls of thinking it was their privilege to "dress loudly . . . to wear large feathers (and perhaps automobile coats) so as to attract the passing glance of the . . . well-dressed young gentleman."[54]

The criticisms apparently went unheeded. In the workplace and on the street, working girls learned that they had rights as well as obligations, and these included the freedom to aspire to American consumerism. Access to money, tempting finery, and new sources of information enabled these girls to fashion their behavior and appearance on their own terms. As the *New York Tribune* asked in 1900, is not it natural for the East Side to "be strictly up to date, for does it not furnish clothes for the rest of the town?"[55] The *Jewish Daily News* came to the same conclusion, noting that because they labored in the garment industry and needle trades, shopgirls developed a "taste and a desire for the 'best'" clothing.[56] Acculturation introduced young women to new rules of consumption where mass-produced goods created a marketplace of material abundance. In this

Right: Young working women knew the importance of dressing stylishly. Below: Window-shoppers gaze at the treasures at Chicago's Marshall Field & Company in 1909.

world of bounty, immigrants measured the attainment of luxuries against the restrictions of the Old Country.[57]

Many newcomers identified ready-made versus homemade as the crucial distinction between the two worlds. In this shift of cultural values, new was better than old, and the machine along with its products were revered. In contrast, homemade styles branded the wearer as a "greenhorn." When asked about her clothing memories, Ida Hananbaum remarked that the clothes she brought with her from Poland in 1923 were homemade whereas her Americanized cousins went to the store and bought their dresses.[58] In her autobiographical novel, *The Promised Land*, Mary Antin includes an evocative account of discovering the "dazzlingly beautiful palace called a 'department store'" where she could exchange her "hateful homemade European costumes . . . for the real American machine-made garments."[59] Similarly, Rose Cohen described the pleasures of her first ready-to-wear outfit:

> I had a new navy blue cashmere dress, the first dress I had ever had, that was not homemade and too large for me, and it cost me a week's wages and many tears. But it was worth it.[60]

Mothers, who spent hours sewing or knitting garments for their children as much out of love as economic necessity, often found their labor rejected by daughters who labeled these homemade styles as inferior. To many younger immigrants, mass-produced clothing became not only a demonstration of upward mobility but also a collective expression of modernity. When seventeen-year-old Eva received a cast-off garment, she wanted the world to know that the coat carried a Wanamaker's label. "I wish I could wear the label on the front," she said.[61]

The immigrants who came to America at the turn of the century arrived at a crucial time in the history of clothing manufacture. The unprecedented expansion of the ready-to-wear

clothing industry in the late nineteenth century played a major role in the rapid shift in American capitalism from an agrarian society to an industrial nation. As Americans moved from a culture of production to a culture of consumption, clothes were more frequently bought than made.[62] From its rather crude beginnings as a service industry for laborers' garments (slop clothes), ready-to-wear developed into a large-scale industry supplying clothing to a mass market. The result was a social leveling that blurred the distinctions between the "haves" and the "have-nots."

Building on the success of the men's ready-to-wear industry, the mass-producers of women's clothing began first with cloaks and outer wraps. Because of the garments' loose shapes, manufacturers could replicate the styling of the fashionable models without concerning themselves with individual fit. Soon, improvements in standardized sizing enabled the industry to expand its line. By the 1890s, corsets, underwear, skirts, and blouses all could be bought "off the rack." Within the next twenty years, virtually every article of female clothing could be purchased ready-made.[63] The layers of fashionable dress, once the exclusive

Above: These women dressed in what became the uniform of working women: shirtwaists and dark tailored skirts.

Opposite: The shirtwaist symbolized the "New Woman." The style was infinitely adaptable and affordable to most women.

domain of the upper class, became accessible to all classes. Wealthy women, who garbed themselves in haute couture ensembles, could cast a critical eye on bargain-basement goods and immediately detect differences in fabric, style, construction, and cut. But to America's new arrivals, the ready-to-wear offerings appeared as an emblem of democracy.

The shirtwaist stands out as the dominant symbol of this new freedom. Patterned after men's shirts, this style became the badge of the "New Woman." It was a staple item, infinitely adaptable to many occasions. And with prices starting as low as thirty-five cents, the shirt-waist was affordable to most women. For those who wanted a fancier version in cotton voile or silk, the styling of the shirtwaist was simple enough that women with minimal sewing skills could fashion their own. On a visit to New York's Educational Alliance, reporter E. C. Erhlich observed a sewing class in progress. One of the foreign-born students, explaining that the lesson for the day was shirtwaists, laid out her "filmy material and trimming" for the visitors. Remarking on her enthusiasm for the project, Erhlich wrote:

> She tells us . . . that since she is learning to sew, she can have three waists for the price of one "store waist" and the garments she makes are prettier and wear longer too.[64]

Sports enthusiasts liked the simple cotton waist for its comfort and freedom of movement, while silk versions, with lacy inserts and frilly ornamentation, seemed the perfect "dress-up" choice. Significantly, it was the working woman who built a wardrobe around the shirtwaist. Symbolizing women's presence in the work force, the shirtwaist was universally worn on the shop floor and the sales floor. Several inexpensive waists combined with a dark-colored tailored skirt enabled working girls to create a functional yet stylish wardrobe. One young immigrant observed "how well dressed and neat were my shop-mates, in their white shirt-waists and dark skirts."[65] Sophie Rosenblum agreed, but she could only afford one waist and dark skirt. Each evening she would washed the blouse out so that it would be fresh for the next workday.[66] In an "Advice to Working Women" column in 1898, the *Jewish Daily News* (the English section of the *Yiddishes Tageblatt*) assured the woman who had to economize, that one good woolen dress with a plain bodice would "do duty all winter," when combined with flannel shirtwaists in the winter and a vest in the fall.[67] For girls like Sadie Frowne, the shirtwaist was indispensable. This sixteen-year-old Jewish garment worker noted that while some of the other factory workers criticized her clothing purchases, stylish dress was a practical investment in her future. "They say that instead of a dollar a week I ought not to spend more than twenty-five cents a week on clothes. . . . But a girl must have clothes if she is to go into society at Ulmer Park or Coney Island or the theater," Sadie explained.[68]

The new avenues of leisure and recreation that Jewish immigrants discovered in America became an important showcase for a girl's expanded wardrobe. While the shirtwaist and simple skirt ably fit the requirements of the work environment, girls wanted more showy outfits when they went out at night. Writing about her experiences in a New York City sweatshop, Elizabeth Hasanovitz described the nightly transformation of her co-workers: "As soon as the power stopped, powder-puffs were extracted from stockings, . . . the aprons changed for the latest style of short hobble-skirts, and off they went to pace Grand Avenue."[69] Experimenting with appearance and self-definition, young working women exchanged the restrained styling of their tailored outfits for bright colors, flashy fabrics, and costume jewelry. The outfits they assembled, more often a parody than an imitation of the elite fashions, asserted their own sense of style.[70] Although Sara in Anzia

Yezierska's novel *Bread Givers* aspired to the "plain beautifulness" of her college peers' simple skirts and sweaters over the more familiar "Grand Street richness," many working-class women rejected the values of understated elegance.[71] From their perspective of consumption, flamboyant finery best expressed their newfound independence.

Young girls came to view work as another avenue of display where a new hair ribbon or a smart lacy waist could provoke admiration and envy. Ida S. remembered that her morning toilette was a time-consuming activity, but she valued appearance more than punctuality. After her brother and cousins helped mold her into the fashionable silhouette by pulling the laces of her corset each morning, she still had to contend with her hair. Creating the "big puffs" always made her five to ten minutes late for work, but Ida would not leave the house until "she fixed her hair properly."[72] Girls dressed for a fashion-wise audience when they went to work; with true adolescent ambiguity, they dressed make an individual statement while striving desperately to conform.

Shopping for these magical products became a major preoccupation of the new arrivals. In Eastern Europe, the acquisition of new clothes traditionally occurred as part of the celebration of the Sabbath and religious holidays. A Russian immigrant who came to America in 1899 at the age of twenty-three recalled the importance of this custom:

> Mother . . . made our clothes by hand. Twice a year, for the special holidays, we would get new clothes. The new clothes would be for Shabbos and the holidays, and the other clothes we would begin to wear for everyday use.[73]

This division collapsed in America, where consumption was a routine part of daily life, and fashions changed from one season to the next. The stylishly dressed could not restrict their purchasing to a religious calendar. Hunting for fashionable goods at affordable prices

Opposite: Shirtwaists came in a variety of styles and price ranges, as shown on this page from Chicago's A.M. Rothschild & Company's catalog of 1900.

Ladies' Shirt Waists

No. 1. Ladies' Waists of Percale, in light and dark colors, double row of insertion in front, and single row in back, new French collar and cuffs. Ordinarily a $1.50 value.
Price.................................$1.00

No. 2. Ladies' Lawn Waists, in all the new and dainty colorings, new French plaited back, double row of embroidery insertion, and full new French collar and cuffs.
Price.................................$1.50

No. 5. Ladies' Plain Tailored Waists, made of corded dimity, French back with 10 tucks, new French collar and cuffs.
Price.................................75c

No. 6. Ladies' Waists of French Chambray, it

No. 9. Another Beauty in Something Entirely New in Ladies' Shirt Waists. It is made of good quality of lawn, entire front tucked, edged with embroidery, new French back, French collars and cuffs.
Price.................................$1.69

No. 10. Ladies Waists in Plain Colored Lawn. These waists have 12 rows of tucking to the back, and the entire front is of all-over lace. A $2.25

Chicago's crowded Milwaukee Avenue Co-op Store in 1906.

turned into an ongoing pursuit. In 1898 a joke appeared in the *Yiddishes Tageblatt* featuring a century-old variation of "shop 'till you drop." Shopping with her mother at a department store on New York City's Sixth Avenue, the daughter noticed a Jewish cemetery at the back of the store. Turning to her mother, she said, "Just think of that for enterprise. . . . If you shop yourself to death, they bury you right here on the premises."[74]

The magnificence of department stores captured the imaginations of newcomers. These utopias of consumption, with their theatrical displays, luxurious interiors, and extravagant appointments, forged an immediate connection between desire and demand. Recognizing that their emporiums attracted customers from all classes, store managers across the country followed Marshall Field's lead and inaugurated the bargain basement. Here shoppers could find discounted merchandise from the main store as well as lower-priced goods made specifically for bargain counters.[75] If these discounted prices were prohibitive, immigrants could at least study the latest fashions and imagine a world of unlimited options. Even though Mina Friedman's clothes were either pushcart goods or handmade, she remembered the thrill of being taken to New York's Siegel Cooper department store by her father. Awed by the "lovely fountain" and colored lights, Mina felt as if she had entered a "fairyland."[76]

For Gertrude Yellin, studying the fashions displayed in Fifth Avenue department stores had tangible benefits: it gained her better employment. When the owner of a sewing establishment discovered Gertrude's designing skills, she took her to stores such as Bonwitt Teller every Saturday. Gertrude was told to "watch these gowns and you come Monday and you do things like this."[77] It was a valuable talent. Evelyn Golbe's boss paid her fifty dollars a week for her work as a copyist. "They would bring in an expensive dress and I would copy it down to a cheaper

line."[78] Living in Chicago, Jennie Schaffner looked to Marshall Field's for her inspiration. "You saw what Field's did, and copied them, and they'd make up some little changes and sell it to the stores," Jennie recalled.[79]

Pushcart vendors offered Jewish shoppers with modest incomes the opportunity to fulfill their increased expectations of consumerism without jeopardizing the family's household budget. "Everyone is looking for a bargain, and everyone has something to sell," observed the *Chicago Tribune* about the city's West Side Jewish street markets.[80] In her study of the spending habits of working girls in 1913, Bertha Jean Richardson noted the trickle-down movement of imitative fashions into the immigrant neighborhoods. She found that on the pushcarts of

Hester Street "ghosts of the real [style] are 'Going, going, gone' for thirty-nine cents."[81] Using the negotiating skills that were essential in the marketplaces of Eastern Europe, Jewish women sought the best bargain. According to Russian immigrant Ilyana Garmisa, "There was no such thing as paying an asking price for anything."[82]

Although these movable stores lacked the luxurious patina of downtown department stores, they satisfied the immigrant's desire for a broad assortment of goods at affordable prices. Unfettered by the expense of rent and high overhead costs, peddlers could reduce their margin of profit and undersell shopkeepers. Many newcomers would hire a wooden pushcart, at the cost of ten cents a day, until

Above: Shoppers outside Chicago's Marshall Field & Company at the turn of the century. The store recognized the needs of its working-class customers by creating the first bargain basement.

*Top and bottom:
Peddlers and shoppers
on the streets of
New York*

they could find a permanent job or establish themselves in some business. Others made the more permanent investment of purchasing a cart for about ten dollars and spending twenty-five dollars a year for a peddling license. Trafficking in new goods or in the "cast-off garments of the middle and upper-lower classes," enterprising peddlers often incorporated modern display techniques to effectively showcase their merchandise.[83] Mannequins, mirrors, folding chairs, and carpets transformed a public street into a semiprivate dressing room. In addition to their up-to-date display strategies, peddlers were persuasive salesmen. Describing the selling techniques of a shoe merchant in 1903, the *Shoe Retailer* credited "the East Side Hebrew's" success to his knowledge of his immigrant customers: "He knows what they will want, puts a price on his wares that his trade can pay, and goes after his customer where he can find them, on the street."[84]

In 1898, the *New York Tribune* estimated that fifteen hundred peddlers operated in the Hester Street vicinity alone.[85] A few years later, the numbers had risen dramatically. In his analysis of the New York City's "pushcart problem" in 1904, Archibald A. Hill reported that police arrested over five thousand peddlers in that year alone. Charges were brought against peddlers who obstructed sidewalks, disturbed the peace with their whistles, or stood in one place for more than thirty minutes.[86] Peddlers became a common sight in all urban immigrant centers. Russian immigrant Bernard Horwich recalled the constant motion of Chicago's peddlers, who traveled from house to house carrying their wares on their backs. "It was not an unusual sight to see hundreds of them . . . in the early morning, spreading throughout the city. There was hardly a streetcar where there were not to be found some Jewish peddlers with their packs."[87] This proliferation of peddlers turned neighborhood streets into small retail centers. "What cannot be bought on the pushcart market on Hester Street cannot be bought in New York," wrote Abraham Cahan. "If you want your goods of a good quality and cheap, Hester Street is the place to buy them."[88]

The number of peddlers increased significantly around the holy days. In Eastern Europe, Passover traditions already incorporated the purchase of new clothing; when combined with the American passion for consumerism, it developed into a major retailing event. In 1907 the socialist newspaper the *Forward* likened the Passover crowd on Grand Street to a "sea of new hats and new dresses" where the "jewelry both genuine and false" reflected "the holiday soul." To accommodate the buying frenzy that occurred during the Passover season, anything with wheels could serve as a pushcart, including "dilapidated baby carriages, children's wagons and even invalids' chairs."[89]

Pushcarts contained an amazing array of merchandise. Street signs in Yiddish, Hebrew, and English announced that everything "from pickled cucumbers to feather beds" could be purchased on the street.[90] Vendors themselves became walking advertisements, filling the neighborhood with their cries of promises and products. E. C. Ehrlich's description of the New York street scene provides a vivid image of the peddler's emporium in 1915:

> We stand . . . bewildered by the noise, the color, the inexpressible feeling of life that vibrates about us. . . . Colors flash upon us from the pushcarts heaped high with gaudy bathing suits and kimonos, from the pails of red peppers and the bunches of bananas, from the very hair ribbons and bright lips of the young girls who pass.[91]

Like the world of the palatial retail stores, which elevated shopping to a feminine social art, the street market became a public arena for women. In 1895 the *New York Tribune* described shoppers on Hester Street as women who are "out to see and be seen as much as to buy." Newcomers who might feel intimidated by the grandeur of department stores could comfortably shop amid the familiar surroundings of their neighborhood. Jewish women discovered a world of goods, attractively presented and modestly priced, just outside their doors. Here they bargained with merchants in their own language, using the purchasing skills they had perfected in Eastern Europe.

In contrast to other ethnic groups, Jewish women came from a culture where they were responsible for the household economy; women in Eastern Europe had a free hand in managing and sustaining the family income. Although the tenets of Judaism limited women's participation in religious worship to the home, married women were encouraged to work outside of the home as part of their familial responsibilities. Their breadwinning labors freed men from the mundane concerns of the secular life, enabling them to focus total attention on the study of the Torah and the Talmud.[92] Yet, even when circumstances dictated a more worldly masculine role, women continued to exert a major force in the marketplace, both as shopkeepers and consumers. Thus Eastern European Jewish women participated in the larger public arena as well as the domestic sphere.

This role shifted somewhat as a result of immigration and the introduction of middle-class ideals. Newcomers discovered the American mandate that wives should avoid wage labor if at all possible. The life of the "lady in the parlor" was beyond the means of most immigrants; by taking in boarders, laundry, and sewing, however, many Jewish women managed to contribute to the family income while technically remaining at home. Of all the immigrant groups that came to America during the years from 1880 to 1924, the Jews had the lowest percentage of married women working outside of the home.[93] Freed from the time constraints of outside employment and no longer limited to the impoverished material offerings of the shtetls and cities of the Pale of

Settlement, Jewish women navigated the ghetto streets, exercising their considerable influence as informed consumers.

In America these women quickly learned that they did not have to limit their tastes to their pocketbook. As historian Andrew Heinze convincingly argues, installment buying "initiated newcomers into the possibilities of immediate acquisition and familiarized them with the impatient optimism" of the American marketplace.[94] Consumers could purchase everything from brass beds to cemetery plots on time payments. Sophonisba Breckenridge found that in the ethnic neighborhoods of Chicago, "buying on credit at the local store is practically universal."[95] Others agreed: "Perhaps nowhere is easy-payment purchasing more elaborately developed than in the West Side Jewish neighborhood," wrote Viola Paradise in 1913.[96] While installment plans offered the newcomers instant possession of products, they could become a seductive trap. Consumers paid higher prices when they succumbed to the lure of "buy now, pay later," and they often found themselves in serious debt. In her study of Jewish working girls in Chicago, Viola Paradise interviewed one girl who said that the credit debts she incurred in her first months in America took her a year and a half to pay off. The author concluded that most of the clothes that the girls buy on installment plans "are usually worn out and are surely out of style before they are paid for."[97]

In addition to installment plans, enterprising retailers did a thriving rental business. Newcomers relied on them particularly for weddings. In Eastern Europe weddings had always been large, festive occasions whose purpose was communal celebration rather than conspicuous consumption. A Jewish immigrant from Bialystok reminisced that her mother attended every village wedding, often wearing the same outfit. "To some weddings she would wear her Sabbath dress and only put a nice

Above: Maxwell Street. Left: These women pose in their borrowed bridesmaid finery.

Opposite: Wedding portrait of Fay Kanter and Manual Cooper, 1917.

shawl on her head," but "better weddings" required borrowing a neighbor's dress.[98] Immigrants modified these traditions upon discovering that the American-style celebration involved great expense. The hall should be filled with a great number of guests enjoying the "music and dancing and wine unlimited," to signal the family's prosperity.[99] Parents willingly denied themselves pleasures, even if it meant going into debt, so that their children could start married life with an elaborate celebration. The *Jewish Daily News* noted in 1898 that:

> A girl who is betrothed is supposed to have a gold watch and chain and a diamond ring as a sign of her engagement. The poorest couple must be married in a hall, even though their furniture is bought on the installment plan.[100]

Typically, bridal costumes were made at home in the Old Country. Writing about her immigration experience for the *Daily Jewish Courier,* Mary Hevash marveled at the longevity of a Galician chuppah dress. For thirty years, Mary's grandmother wore her black satin wedding dress on special occasions; the fabric then "spent its . . . declining, veteran years on my grandfather's back in the shape of a caftan."[101] In contrast, American tradition decreed that the wedding clothes, not only for the bride and groom but also for the attendants and guests, should be elaborate ensembles that followed the latest trends. Rosa Schneiderman used the "new affluence" of her six-dollar-a-week job as a lining-maker to purchase a dress to wear to a co-worker's wedding. After years of wearing poorly made clothes, this new dress of "pearly gray with a deep bertha [collar] of ecru lace lined in pink" gave her great pleasure and was worth the expense.[102] But these symbols did not come cheaply. While store-window mannequins who "appear ready to be led to the altar" beckoned irresistibly, in their "white satin and bridal veils," the garments they modeled carried a hefty price tag.[103] Before she married, Ida S. lived in three rooms with six other

people; nonetheless, her wedding, she insisted, had to special. Saving for months, Ida ordered the dress of her dreams, "all beaded and all beautiful." The dressmaker received eighty dollars and some free advertising. She kept the dress in her shop window for a month before the wedding and "all the girls would walk by and admire it."[104] Some newcomers chose to rent the accoutrements of a showy wedding rather than do without. The *Jewish Daily News*

Sophie Sobel and Charles Hopp on their wedding day, c. 1890.

reminded its readers that because of the practical economy of these rental houses, "poverty is no excuse for the absence of a shining satin dress with bridal bouquet and veil."[105]

In 1905, the *Boston Advocate* reported on a number of "quaint little shops" on New York's Lower East Side that catered to the bride and groom who wanted the status of a luxury wedding without the prohibitive costs. Tableware, decorations, wedding cakes (which could be admired but not eaten), and even guests all could be hired at a small expense. And rather than spending sleepless nights debating the merits of Irish versus Valenciennes lace trimming, a poor working girl need waste "neither time nor energy in selecting clothes"; instead she could wait until the morning of her wedding day to rent her wedding gown.[106]

Whether rented, purchased, or handmade, American clothing seemed to be the inevitable first step in the immigrants' adjustment to their new homeland. Anxious to shed the label of greenhorn, Jewish women scrimped and saved to acquire alluring modern fashions. Their voices articulate the internal desire and external pressure to "look American"; later they would also reverberate with the consequences of refashioning one's visible self. But in the initial shock of transition, many women seized upon a change of clothes to symbolize their new American consciousness. Their reactions to the prevailing fashions expressed their individual responses to the collective assimilation experience. Filled with dreams of making a new life, enthralled with the promises of capitalism, and bombarded with messages about appearance and behavior, many Jewish women took off their wigs and put on the cloak of America.

Notes

1. Abraham Cahan, *Yekl, A Tale of the New York Ghetto* (New York: 1896), 34–37.

2. Ida Feldman, Ellis Island Oral History Project, Ellis Island Immigration Museum.

3. Viola Paradise, "The Jewish Immigrant Girl in Chicago," *Survey,* September 6, 1913, 703–04.

4. Dr. Morris Moel, Ellis Island Oral History Project.

5. Lucjan Dobroszycki and Barbara Kirshenblatt-Gimblett, *Image Before My Eyes: A Photographic History of Jewish Life in Poland, 1864–1939* (New York: 1977), xiii.

6. Gill Sherrid, Ellis Island Oral History Project.

7. Susan A. Glenn, *Daughters of the Shtetl: Life and Labor in the Immigrant Generation* (Ithaca: 1990), 2.

8. U. S. Industrial Commission Report, vol. 14, 126.

9. Ida Ellis, Ellis Island Oral History Project.

10. S.P. Breckenridge, *New Homes for Old* (New York: 1921), 45.

11. Arthur Hertzberg, *The Jews in America: Four Centuries of an Uneasy Alliance: A History* (New York: 1989), 172.

12. Anna Kuthan, New York City Immigrant Labor History Project, Tamiment Library, New York University.

13. Interview with Rose Jaffee, 1965, courtesy of Richard Jaffee.

14. Tape I-81, New York City Immigrant Labor History Project.

15. Max and Milton Shatsky, Ellis Island Oral History Project.

16. Mina K. Friedman, "Time About No News to All," unpublished manuscript, courtesy of Alan Friedman.

17. Sara J. Abrams, "Things Trivial," American Jewish Autobiographies Collection, #92, YIVO Archives, YIVO Institute for Jewish Research.

18. Interview with Sophie Abrams, Oral History Project of the City University of New York, quoted in Elizabeth Ewen, *Immigrant Women in the Land of Dollars: Life and Culture on the Lower East Side, 1890–1925* (New York: 1985), 68.

19. "Woman's Crowning Glory," *Boston Advocate,* June 2, 1905.

20. Lois Banner, *American Beauty* (New York: 1983), 208–209.

21. Sally Goldstein, interview with Carla Reiter and Joanne Grossman.

22. Hutchins Hapgood, *The Spirit of the Ghetto* (New York, 1902; reprint, Cambridge, Mass.: 1967), 72–73.

23. Paradise, "The Jewish Immigrant Girl in Chicago," 704.

24. "The Wig: In the Past and In the Present," *Di Froyen-Velt*, November 1913, 1–4.

25. Charlotte Baum, Paula Hyman, and Sonya Michel, *The Jewish Women in America* (New York: 1975), 205.

26. "All Right! Hurry Up," in Moses Rischin, *Grandma Never Lived in America: The New Journalism of Abraham Cahan* (Bloomington, Ind.: 1985), 143.

27. Ida Ellis, Ellis Island Oral History Project.

28. Giza Frankel, "Notes on the Costume of the Jewish Woman in Eastern Europe," *Journal of Jewish Art*, 7 (1980): 50–57.

29. *New York Tribune, Illustrated Supplement*, August 26, 1900, reprinted in Jacob Rader Marcus, *The American Jewish Woman: A Documentary History* (New York: 1981), 198–99.

30. Abraham Cahan, *The Imported Bridegroom and Other Tales of the New York Ghetto* (New York: 1898; reprint, New York: 1970), 112.

31. Doris Weatherford, *Foreign & Female: Immigrant Women in America, 1840–1930* (New York: 1986), 97.

32. Anzia Yezierska, *Bread Givers* (Garden City, New York; reprint, New York: 1975), 2.

33. From a scrapbook courtesy of Marilyn Golden.

34. Lillian Wald, *House on Henry Street* (1915; reprint, New York: 1971), 193, quoted in Ewen, *Immigrant Women in the Land of Dollars*, 200.

35. Celia Adler, Ellis Island Oral History Project.

36. Rose Cohen, *Out of the Shadows* (New York: 1918), 51.

37. Elizabeth Repshsis, Ellis Island Oral History Project.

38. Breckenridge, *New Homes for Old*, 174.

39. "Life of Orthodox Jewish Girls in the Smaller Cities, Part II," *Jewish Daily News*, March 25, 1898.

40. *Shoe Retailer*, September 16, 1903, 168.

41. Fannie Shoock, Ellis Island Oral History Project.

42. Rose R., New York City Immigrant Labor History Project, I-55.

43. Rose Schneiderman, *All For One* (New York: 1967) reprinted in Irving Howe and Kenneth Libo, *How We Lived: A Documentary History of Immigrant Jews in America, 1880–1930* (New York: 1979), 132.

44. Charlotte Baum, Paula Hyman, and Sonya Michel, *The Jewish Woman in America*, 222–25.

45. Yezierska, *Bread Givers*, 30.

46. Gertrude Yellin, Ellis Island Oral History Project.

47. Andrew Heinze, *Adapting to Abundance: Jewish Immigrants, Mass Consumption, and the Search for Human Identity* (New York: 1990), 57.

48. "Styles and Fashions," *Di Froyen-Velt*, June 1913, 8.

49. *Jewish Daily News*, August 22, 1898.

50. Jane Addams, "The Subtle Problems of Charity," *Atlantic Monthly*, 83 (February 1899): 168.

51. Andria Taylor Hourwich and Gladys Palmers, eds., *I Am a Woman Worker* (1936; reprint, New York: 1974), 22–36.

52. "Autobiography of a Shop Girl," *Frank Leslie's Popular Monthly*, 61 (May 1903): 58.

53. "Talks with My Sister," *Jewish Daily News*, December 7, 1900.

54. "The Observer," *Jewish Daily News*, January 13, 1902.

55. *New York Tribune, Illustrated Supplement*, reprinted in Jacob Rader Marcus, *The American Jewish Woman*, 499.

56. "The Observer," *Jewish Daily News*, January 13, 1902.

57. Eva Morawski, "For Bread with Butter: Life-Worlds of Peasant Immigrants from Eastern Central Europe, 1880–1914," *Journal of Social History*, Spring 1984: 396.

58. Ida Hanenbaum, Ellis Island Oral History Project.

59. Mary Antin, *The Promised Land* (Boston: 1912), 187.

60. Cohen, *Out of the Shadow*, 129.

61. Elisabeth Howe Bliss, "Intimate Studies in the Lives of Fifty Working Class Girls," (master's thesis, Columbia University, 1915), 29.

62. Stuart and Elizabeth Ewen, *Channels of Desire: Mass Images and the Shaping of American Consciousness* (New York: 1982), 160–61.

63. Barbara Clark Smith and Kathy Peiss, *Men and Women: A History of Costume, Gender, and Power* (Washington, D.C.: 1989), 49.

64. E.C. Ehrlich, "A Tour of New York Jewishly Conducted, Part III," *Sentinel*, September 15, 1916.

65. Sydelle Kramer and Jenny Masur, eds., *Jewish Grandmothers* (Boston: 1976).

66. Interview with Annette Grafman.

67. "Advice to Working Women," *Jewish Daily News*, December 2, 1898.

68. Hamilton Holt, ed., *Stories of Undistinguished Americans as Told by Themselves* (New York: 1906), 46.

69. Elizabeth Hasanovitz, *One of Them: Chapters from a Passionate Autobiography* (Boston: 1918), 93.

70. Lois Banner, *American Beauty* (New York: 1983), 198–99.

71. Yezierska, *Bread Givers*, 212.

72. Interview with Ida S., New York City Immigrant Labor History Project.

73. Margaret Mead Papers, Research in Contemporary Cultures, vol. 5, J-R 44, August 19, 1947, Library of Congress.

74. *Yiddishes Tageblatt*, April 20, 1898.

75. Heinze, *Adapting to Abundance*, 111.

76. Friedman, "Time About No News To All."

77. Gertrude Yellin, Ellis Island Oral History Project.

78. Evelyn Golbe, Ellis Island Oral History Project.

79. Jennie Schaffner, inteview with Eden Rosenbush, June 19,1993.

80. Chicago *Tribune*, July 19, 1891, cited in Melvin G. Holli and Peter d'A. Jones, *Ethnic Chicago* (Grand Rapids, Mich.: 1984), 84.

81. Bertha Jean Richardson, *The Woman Who Spends: A Study of Her Economic Function* (Boston: 1913), 75–77.

82. Ilyana Garmisa, interview with Eden Rosenbush.

83. "Tageblatt Park," *Jewish Daily News*, November 20, 1919.

84. *The Shoe Retailer*, September 16, 1903, 168.

85. "Thursday in Hester Street," *New York Tribune*, September 15, 1898.

86. Archibald A. Hill, "The Pushcart Peddlers of New York," *Independent,* 61 (1904): 916.

87. Bernard Horwich, *My First Eighty Years* (Chicago: 1939), 126.

88. Abraham Cahan, "Pushcarts Full of Woe," June 29, 1898, in Moses Rischin, ed., *Grandma Never Lived in America*: *The New Journalism of Abraham Cahan* (Bloomington: 1985), 261.

89. Hill, "The Pushcart Peddlers of New York," 919.

90. Edward A. Steiner, "The Russian and Polish Jew in New York," *Outlook*, November 1, 1902, 530.

91. Ehrlich, "A Tour of New York."

92. Heinze, *Adapting to Abundance*, 105–06.

93. Paula E. Hyman, "Culture and Gender: Women in the Immigrant Jewish Community," in David Berger, ed., *Legacy of Jewish Immigration: 1881 and Its Impact* (New York: 1983), 157–62.

94. Heinze, *Adapting to Abundance*, 57.

95. Breckenridge, *New Homes for Old*, 124.

96. Paradise, "The Jewish Immigrant Girl in Chicago," 702.

97. Paradise, "The Jewish Immigrant Girl in Chicago," 702–03.

98. Margaret Mead Papers, Research in Contemporary Cultures, G46, J-P 132.

99. *New York Tribune Illustrated Supplement*, June 30, 1901, 4.

100. "Life of Orthodox Jewish Girls," *Jewish Daily News*, March 25, 1898.

101. Mary Hevash, "My Father and I: Part Two," *The Daily Jewish Courier*, October 14, 1920.

102. Rose Schneiderman with Lucy Goldthwaite, *All for One* (New York: 1967), 35–46.

103. Erhlich, "A Tour of New York."

104. Ida S., New York City Immigrant Labor History Project.

105. M. J. McKenna, "Our Brethren in the Ghetto," *Jewish Daily News*, March 3, 1899.

106. "Borrowed Finery," *Boston Advocate*, December 15, 1905.

In the Old World, finery, such as the embroidered pinafore (below), was often reserved for the Sabbath and holidays. In the New World, immigrants purchased garments, such as hats and shirtwaists, to parade their identities as Americans.

This two-piece afternoon outfit would have been right in the fashion mainstream around 1912, when Jennie Rosenberg Frankfort bought it in Chicago.

Fannie Addis wore this smart silk and wool swimsuit on the beaches of South Haven, Michigan, where she vacationed with her husband c. 1917. The suit's Marshall Field's label put Fannie at the forefront of fashion.

Sophie Benet Kanter emigrated from Russia in the 1890s. Her daughter, Fay, who was born in America, wore this dress when she graduated from Oliver Goldsmith School in Chicago in 1907.

The label on this flannel and lace confection identifies it as the creation of "Madame Grossman, Logan Square." Its owner, Clara Olenick Gordon, came from Mariompol, Russia, to Chicago around 1889.

CASTLE GARDEN EMIGRANT-CATCHER

Greening Out

This cartoon depicts the potential dangers awaiting new arrivals at Castle Garden, the point of entry for immigrants before Ellis Island opened in 1892.

When sixteen-year-old Celia left Eastern Europe to live with her uncle in Brooklyn, she was overjoyed. She looked forward to her grand adventure, believing that "everyone in America was a friend of strangers."[1] But when Celia landed, she discovered that living in America did not automatically make you American. Like so many other immigrants who were identified as foreigners and branded as aliens, Celia quickly discovered her marginal status as a *grueneheim*, the Yiddish word for greenhorn. The label conjures up the uncertainty and condescension that awaited recent immigrants and speaks to the pressures they must have felt to conform. Sara Abrams remembered "greenhorn" as the first English word she heard after she landed in New York. "They used to spot a 'green-horn' like a monkey does a louse," she wrote.[2] After struggling and sacrificing for months, even years, to reach American soil, the immigrants were met with a welcome that was tinged with derision.

All newcomers had to endure the indignity of greenhorn status. Long before they had contact with mainstream America, newcomers heard the taunting cry from within their own ethnic community. Rose Krawetz remembered all "the things you go through when you're a greenhorn and you come in. And they looked down on you, although they were greenhorns themselves."[3] For established immigrants, labeling someone else as a greenhorn was a way of marking progress, because by separating themselves from the mistakes of the newcomer they rose a notch on the assimilation ladder. Nowhere is this more apparent than in

91

the immigrant theater. The Yiddish theater, which dealt so skillfully and successfully with all aspects of the immigrant experience, routinely showcased the greenhorn as part of its repertoire of stock characters. Delighted audiences could howl at the confusion of the greenhorn character and take comfort in the knowledge that those days of initiation were behind them.[4] It was laughter full of sympathetic recognition.

Within the intimate environment of a Yiddish theater and viewed from the safe distance of the footlights, the greenhorn's misadventures provided great entertainment.[5] Yet the pain of being cast as an outsider was real. Ruth Katz left Poland at the age of sixteen with her sister as her only companion. When the girls reached Baltimore to meet friends of the family, Ruth discovered that their arrival piqued the interest of numerous inquiring minds. "The girlfriends of the girl of the people that I came to, they all came to look at the greenhorns." One of them asked to see Ruth's stockings, eager to know "if greenhorns wear stockings with all different colors."[6]

Jewish immigrants found the label of greenhorn an especially onerous burden since they, more than any other group, saw their migration as permanent. Eager to establish a place for themselves in their newly adopted country and longing to shed the ignoble status of the greenhorn, Jews worked to "green themselves out." If they wanted to fit in, they had to make changes. Still reeling from the initial trauma of resettlement, immigrants quickly identified the Old World customs that jeopardized their acceptance in America.

Max Shatsky summarized the conflicting messages he received when he first arrived. Other children called him greenhorn as "a thing that was meant to get your goat. So I was confused. Here people were welcoming us with open arms, on the other hand others coming around saying we didn't belong here, or we're

The American Yiddish theater often presented plays about the experiences of greenhorns. Plays such as The Green Millionaire poked fun at the new arrivals.

This woman's bulky clothing, kerchief, sturdy shoes, and bundle immediately identify her as a greenhorn.

greenhorns."[7] Celia Adler recalled similar treatment. Sent by her parents to live with friends, Celia arrived in America alone at the age of twelve. When the family instructed their son to take Celia to the dressmaking shop where she would be working, the boy did little to hide his embarrassment over being seen with a greenhorn. He told Celia, "If you see my friends, go behind me."[8] Minnie Publicker captured the humiliation of discovering that her greenhorn dress was not what "real" Americans wore. The dress was lovingly made by her mother, who wanted to create special outfits to celebrate Minnie's and her sister's first day of school in America. When she saw the American flag, she knew she had found her inspiration. Using red, white, and blue fabric, she made "buster brown dresses for us using stars for the collar— stripes for the pleats." Minnie thought her dress was beautiful until she heard the taunting jeers of her classmates. They laughed so hard that Minnie crouched into a corner of the school yard and cried. The principal explained "what the American flag was worth" and steered her out through the back door so that she could go home and change.[9]

Being a greenhorn made Sarah Rothman more than an object of scorn: it made her a target of discrimination. For her first six months in America, Sarah and her husband and child lived with her sister's family. Seven people crowded into cramped quarters was not easy, but moving out also presented problems. Sarah discovered that her brother-in-law's signature was the only one the landlord trusted. He said, "'They are greenhorns. Maybe they won't make a living. You better sign the lease.' I used to be mad when they used to call me green. I said, 'How long does it take it not to be green?'"[10]

A reasonable question, but difficult to answer. "Greening out" was a gradual process and widely interpreted, but it was universally understood that clothing was the first step. Fannie Friedman's father instructed his family not to speak Yiddish on the train ride to their new home in Boston so that others would not recognize them as newcomers. But Fannie knew better. "Everybody knew, the way we were dressed, they knew we were immigrants."[11] The message was clear—looking American was an absolute necessity for successful adjustment.

For Ludmila Foxlee, the renovation of immigrants' dress needed to begin as soon as they touched American soil. Working for the Department for Foreign-born Women and Immigration of the YWCA, she established an office on Ellis Island in 1920. Together with other social workers, Foxlee provided assistance to recent émigrés; part of their work included operating a clothing store. In her memoirs, Foxlee recorded numerous case studies documenting the results of her work. In some instances, the primary concern was practical: a Polish woman who arrived wearing a cotton dress and badly worn coat left the island warmly clothed in a woolen dress and "old-fashioned black plush coat." For other women, a change of clothes helped disguise their greenhorn status. When Zofia F. arrived from Russia to join her husband, the social worker detected a bad haircut partially hidden by the folds of an "immense white woolen shawl." A fellow traveler told her "she could not proceed looking like that" and cut and arranged Zofia's hair in an "artistic" style. Foxlee then offered her a small hat that Zofia "gladly accepted when I told her that the shawl would mark her as a newcomer at first sight." (Although fashionable today, at the turn of the century shawls were considered the garment of poor, working-class women.) Foxlee admitted that not all immigrants welcomed such advice, however well-intentioned. Some women found the changes too startling and requested the familiarity of their old clothes.[12]

Foxlee tried to arrange these transformations with an eye on cultural differences. She understood, for example, that despite what

Below: Social workers sometimes provided recent immigrants with American clothing.

Before and After

This illustration accompanied an article by Ludmila Foxlee concerning the importance of a changed appearance for immigrant women.

fashion dictated in 1923, a "mid-European peasant woman would have been uneasy under a layer of rouge on her cheeks and powder on her nose and would probably have resented such treatment."[13] She also made it clear that for her efforts to be successful, a change of clothes had to be part of a larger assimilation effort. Noting that sometimes an immigrant girl thinks the process stops with a haircut and fashionable dresses, hats, and shoes, Foxlee stressed the importance of community outreach and American schooling. "We can say that learning English seemed to us the most important undertaking for the new arrivals . . . if . . . a sense of security, of belonging to this new world, was to be established."[14]

Foxlee and the Immigrant Social Service were concerned with more than physical comfort; they also addressed the role clothing played in the immigrant family's psychological needs. As she reported in her memoirs, "After ten years of separation, these toil-worn peasant women seemed to have few attractive qualities in the eyes of their men."[15] Concerned with the strain this might place on marital reunions, Foxlee tried to Americanize women immigrants before they left Ellis Island. Marie Z. arrived at Ellis Island in her native Russian costume of an embroidered black wool skirt, peacock blue sweater, and heavy flannel drawers, which left her wilting in the July heat. Foxlee exchanged the sweltering wool for thin underwear and a cotton traveling dress. "Thus clothed she was ready to face" her husband who, after a sixteen-year separation, was "virtually a stranger to her."[16]

Others agreed with Foxlee's assessment that "10 or 15 years in America made a good deal of difference in a man's ideal of womanhood." David Blaustein, head of the Educational Alliance, attributed the alarming number of divorces among Jews living on the Lower East Side to the cultural disparities between "Americanized" husbands and their "greenhorn" wives:

The man comes to this country first. Five years later, during which time he had lived as a single man, he sends for his wife. He finds her not five years behind him, but two centuries. He has acquired a new language, new clothes and customs, and a new country. He finds the union insupportable.[17]

Yiddish playwright Kobrin wrote a comedy, *The Nextdoor Neighbors*, that explored this aspect of the immigrant experience. After living alone in America for two years, Willy pictures himself a changed man. Trying to explain to his wife why they are no longer a couple, he says: "Hindele . . . I am Willy, do you understand? Without a beard. And I do not pray, and I eat milk and meat dishes from the same plate—and you are pious!" But more than kosher food separates the couple. Willy has changed his taste in

Immigrants stepped off the boat clutching all that remained of their lives in Europe.

An English class at New York's Educational Alliance.

women, and it is Clara, his neighbor's wife and the "picture of the American lady," who earns his admiration. All is not lost, however; Hindele adopts a new hairstyle and a fashionable dress, and Willy seeks a reconciliation. [18]

In real life, however, many women émigrés struggled with the demands that their Americanized husbands placed on them. In her autobiographical novel, *The Promised Land*, Mary Antin presents a haunting portrait of her mother's agonizing decision to redefine herself. This Orthodox woman, who every Sabbath "replaced the cotton kerchief by the well-brushed wig," came to America only to discover that her husband was no longer observant.[19] And worse, he insisted that his wife follow his example. Antin writes of her mother's painful abandonment of her beliefs. She "gradually divested herself, at my father's bidding, of the mantle of orthodox observance,

but the process cost her many a pang, because the fabric of that venerable garment was interwoven with the fabric of her soul."[20]

The symbolism of a change of clothes resonated deeply within the Jewish community. It proclaimed the newcomer as a prospective citizen and celebrated the long-awaited entry into the land of promise. In 1902, the *Forward* interviewed a photographer who played a critical role in the immigrant's rite of passage. He described the greenhorns who came to his studio to pose for portraits. Usually accompanied by friends or relatives and often just off the boat, Jewish immigrants arrived wearing their new American clothing. The photographer kept a stock supply of jewelry and watches that the client could borrow as props if he or she had yet to acquire these emblems of prosperity. The image would then be sent back to relatives in Europe as proof of the immigrant's instant success.[21]

In one memorable instance, a photograph failed to produce the desired response. In 1908, Jennie Schaffner left her parents behind to come to America. Just fifteen years old, she traveled from Russia to Chicago, where she got a job making buttonholes. Although it was "the most boring job you could think of," the factory provided Jennie with an inner circle of close friends. They quickly became her sartorial advisers, helping her make her first American dress and introducing her to the shaping wizardry of a corset. The results were so pleasing that Jennie decided to have a picture taken of her "new" self wearing her finery and an oversized starched hairbow to send back home to her mother. But instead of awe, Jennie received admonishment. Taking one look at the photograph, Jennie's mother wrote back and told her to take the ironing board off of her head.[22]

And so Jewish women, some out of necessity and others out of desire, began to conform to a new dress code. Edward Steiner reported in 1902 that "the 'greener' is treated with kindness, but is made to feel his greenness at every point." He went on to observe that immediately upon arrival, Eastern European immigrants went through *ausgreenen*, an adjustment period during which they "shed old-country clothes and habits . . . becoming like us."[23] Similarly, Horace Kallen noted in his 1915 defense of cultural pluralism that the three keys to Americanization were adopting American clothes and manners, learning English, and embracing American political attitudes. Of these, Kallen contended that "clothes and manners" were the most easily acquired, noting that "in these days of ready-made clothing . . . it is almost impossible that the [masses] . . . should wear other than uniform clothes."[24]

But did they? Certainly easy credit, bargain-priced goods, and the explosion of mass-marketed products placed "American" clothing within the reach of all but the poorest Jews. But grasping the complexities of a new fashion sys-

Rose Maremont wore the large starched bow that was popular among girls in the early twentieth century.

Many immigrants sent studio photographs to friends and relatives back home to display their newfound prosperity.

tem requires knowledge of both the tangible and intangible details of taste, fashion, and etiquette. Sensing what is wrong is different from knowing what is right. It is a fine distinction requiring a certain level of consumer sophistication, and, as journalist Hutchins Hapgood explained, a monumental task given the complexity of American cultural conventions. He wrote, "Jewish women lack the subtle charm of the American woman, who is full of feminine devices, complicated flirtatiousness, who in her dress and personal appearance seeks the plastic epigram."[25]

As they navigated their way through the unfamiliar territory of a new standard of femininity and tried to sort through the maze of American goods, Jewish women looked to others for assistance. And there was plenty to be found. Teachers, employers, bureaucrats, and social workers entreated immigrants to join America's melting pot and offered to show them the way. Yiddish newspapers, etiquette manuals, and magazines proffered their opinions on American styles to the newcomers. Listening to this cacophony of advice, immi-

ETIQUETTE

Compiled by TASHRAK.

Copyright 1912 by the Hebrew Publishing Co., New York.

Left: Etikete *(Etiquette)
by Tashrak guided new
Jewish immigrants
through the rules of
proper behavior in
their native language.
The author discussed
topics such as how to
dress and how to flirt.*

These two Lithuanian
Jews were no longer
"green" in their stylish
hats, shirtwaists, and
tailored skirts.

grants could not help but emit a groan of confusion. But sifting through the advice of the
"experts" would come later. In those all-
important first weeks of resettlement, newcomers relied on family, neighbors, and
landsleit to guide their transition from greenhorn to American.

With memories of their own fears and
mishaps still fresh in their minds, established
immigrants took the greenhorns under their
wings, providing guidance, practical tips, and
hand-me-down clothing. Their generosity
made them experts in the eyes of the newcomers. In tenement houses and ghetto neighborhoods, established Jews shared coping
strategies with the new arrivals, providing a
much-needed antidote to their overwhelming
sense of alienation and loneliness.[26] Under the
tutelage of their more experienced landsleit,
newly landed immigrants learned where to
shop and what to buy. Without such assis-

tance, greenhorns often became victims of unscrupulous shopkeepers. Anna Kuthan told the story of her first shopping expedition in America. Recognizing that she needed to "dress myself a little bit decent," Anna walked into a Czech clothing store. Inexperienced with market prices and bargaining practices, Anna willingly paid the quoted price of forty dollars only to discover "the next day it was worth less than 18 dollars."[27]

Recalling his arrival from Russia in 1902, Max Grossman said, "You came together with your own group. . . . They found a place for you to live and a place for you to work."[28] Joined by a common language and shared customs,

Ethnic neighborhoods were a haven for newly arrived immigrants.

immigrants found a familiar haven within their own ethnic community. Isidore Wisotsky remembered the kindness of a neighbor, Mrs. Katz, who showed his mother around the neighborhood. She offered an insider's guide to installment buying and introduced Mrs. Wisotsky to the local butcher and grocer, admonishing them to give her quality food at fair prices. "To Mother she said, 'Buy with open eyes.'" A visit from Isidore's Aunt Rose and Uncle Nathan yielded more dramatic advice. After a tearful reunion, Rose said, "And now, greenhorns, you must drink a glass of water and epsom salt. I brought this along to wash out your insides so you will be cleansed in America."[29] Lucy Lang

also had to reason to wish her purification could be spiritual. After twenty-three days aboard ship, Lucy, her siblings, and her mother finally reached New York City. No sooner had they arrived at the apartment where her father was living than Lucy's Aunt Chaye appeared with advice on her lips and castor oil in her hand. "She ordered each of us to take a dose because we were greenhorns and must purge Europe from our systems."[30]

For Lillian Gorenstein, it was a family friend who helped her family assimilate into American society:

> Mrs. Cohen . . . took it upon herself to help us become Americanized. . . . She didn't care whether one liked America or not. We were in America, no? And the sooner we became Americans the better. No sooner did we unpack than she took it upon herself to teach Ma all about American housekeeping. She . . . took all of us to Mr. Walper's store on Broadway where we were outfitted with new clothes and shoes. In my new dress and hairdo in the American style, I looked like I was thirty years of age instead of fifteen.

But immigrants were not blank slates just waiting for America's imprint. While understanding the importance of these initiation rites as expressions of their new identities, they still weighed the merits of such advice against their own values. Mrs. Cohen discovered her protégée's limits when she tried to squeeze Lillian into a corset. Once Lillian returned home she tried on the corset, then took it off forever. "I told Ma to tell Mrs. Cohen that I would be a good American without wearing a corset," she asserted.[31]

For Sara Abrams, visiting relatives was a crucial part of assimilation because it provided her with an opportunity to observe "how people lived, how they acted and reacted." Memorizing every detail of their "modern" home, she accepted their affluence as a fact of life because "they were 'Americans.'" Other well-to-do relatives offered Sara a tantalizing image of American consumerism. They wore dresses made from patterns and high-top white shoes and owned

Shop windows displayed tantalizing merchandise on New York's Lower East Side.

scarves and muffs. But most impressive was the picture of George Washington displayed proudly on an easel in their living room. Sara recalled, "To me, it meant the height of achievement."[32]

Sara's precise recording of images and details was typical. Long before they learned the language of their new home, immigrants absorbed the details of their new surroundings through careful observation. When asked where she developed her craving for beautiful clothes, Ida Richter explained: "I saw people who looked better and dressed better, and I wanted to be like that kind. They were Americans, naturally [and] I wanted to be an American, very much."[33]

Immigrants interested in an aesthetic education just had to walk outside; the street scene functioned as an immediate classroom for these "urban pioneers."[34] When Anuta Sharrow arrived in Chicago in 1919 she thought she had reached paradise; despite "all kinds of shortcomings . . . everything was in abundance."[35] For Jennie Matyas it was the sight of other children wearing both shoes and stockings that symbolized the bountiful offerings of her new home. She first saw this wonderful sight when she landed in New York City in September 1905. Bewildered at such luxury, Jennie concluded that she must have arrived on a special day in America, but her father corrected her. "It is no holiday at all," he said. Jenny was amazed at his ignorance. "Imagine, he's lived in this country two years now and he doesn't know that it must be a holiday because how else would the children be allowed to wear shoes and stockings? If it weren't a holiday they'd be barefoot."[36]

Advertisements punctuated the city environment with pictures and promotional appeals "bringing the beautiful within the reach of all."[37] Storefront displays and fashionably dressed mannequins brought the static printed images to life. City thoroughfares became moving billboards as attractively arranged merchandise beckoned irresistibly from large plate-glass windows.[38] The magnetic display of new products and promises pulled immigrants into a new cycle of consumption from the moment they entered the street.[39] Window-shopping was more than diversion; it was an agent of acculturation. Ella Wolf credited her newfound sense of stylishness to the long walks she took on the Sabbath. "I would see all the big stores. . . . I was too shy to go inside, just to look. But the window shoppings taught me a great deal."[40]

While the department stores relied on the seductive appeal of their merchandise to lure shoppers, neighborhood shops in the heart of ethnic communities used more aggressive marketing techniques. Owners often hired hawkers to initiate sales; if the merchandise did not grab you, a "puller-in" would. Writing about her first experience as a "hayseed" walking down New York City's Division Street, also known as "Millinery Row," Rose Pastor presented a daunting picture. Having escaped the clutches of one "puller-in," Rose incorrectly assumed that she was safe:

> I saw the "puller-in" at the next shop, but I supposed that she, having witnessed the failure of her contemporary, would let me pass in peace. But, alas! there was no passing in anything but pieces, for . . . I was caught by the sleeve of my coat and the folds of my skirt by a pair of strong hands and heard a hard voice say in a very foreign English: "Here, lady, dis is de vay to buy a het . . . yes, you must come in here; this is the only place where you can buy a nice black hat for a dollar forty-seven cents—honestly!"[41]

Seduced by retailers, pressured by relatives, and eager to hasten their metamorphosis from "Yidn to Yankee," Jewish women worked to acquire the trappings of American femininity. But the superabundance of available goods made their pursuit of fashion both easier and more difficult. The same explosion of mass-produced items that promised a world of opportunity also added a new layer of complexity to

Above: Fashionably dressed mannequins beckon irresistibly from clothing shops. Right: Stylish New Yorkers stroll down a city street.

the shopping expedition. As they built a new wardrobe, piece by precious piece, immigrants had to make choices that required an insider's knowledge of the system. It was within the immediate family that most women acquired their initial understanding of "greening out," but once they settled in, a chorus of advisors joined the familial voices in offering advice.

During the Progressive Era, social reformers considered the plight of urban dwellers with increasing alarm. Their efforts to improve living and working conditions gave rise to numerous cultural agencies that incorporated the education of immigrants into their larger mission. The settlement-house movement began when Jane Addams established Hull-House on Chicago's West Side in 1889. Others soon followed, providing immigrants with vocational training, medical services, and cultural instruction. Newcomers who went to settlement

houses to study English and citizenship could also learn about cooking, hygiene, and home economics. Mina Friedman used to go to Christadora House in Brooklyn after school, where she was served household tips along with her hot cocoa. "We would bring a piece of our clothing and were given a washtub full of hot soapy water and a wash board; after washing the garment we would hang it up to dry and the next day we would iron it." Mina recalled that the classes often caught the attention of wealthy ladies. They would come to the settlement house "to watch us sew and approve that we slum children were being taught the skills appropriate to our station in life; to be housewives or . . . servants."[42]

The unmistakable tone of condescension that Mina detected in her ladies bountiful was not unique. It was fine to help the underprivileged as long as they knew their place and

Young Jewish immigrants learned cooking at the Brooklyn Vocational School (above) and sewing skills at the Jewish Training School (opposite).

dressed accordingly. Ellen Richardson, the founding leader of the domestic science movement, wrote of her shock that the poor tenement girls did not look poor. She asked:

> Did you ever go down to one of the city settlements full of the desire to help and lift up the poor shop girl? There must be some mistake, you thought. . . . They looked better dressed than you did. Plumes on their heads, a rustle of silk petticoats, everything about them in the latest style.[43]

Jane Addams, however, understood that for the immigrant girl who aimed higher than the tenement world of her parents, stylish dress was the best road to advancement. With "little social standing," this girl "knows full well how much habit and style of dress have to do with her position. . . . If social advancement is her aim, it is the most sensible thing which she can do."[44] Addams also recognized that "working girls" and "young ladies" interpreted stylishness very differently. For the factory or shop girl, "putting on the style" was often her first attempt at belonging. Addressing charity workers who had been raised to consider it vulgar to expend excessive amounts of money or attention on one's appearance, Addams urged them to view such behavior as part of a different social consciousness:

> The poor naturally try to bridge the difference by reproducing the street clothes which they have seen; they therefore imitate, sometimes in more showy and often in more trying colors, in cheap and flimsy materials, in poor shoes and flippant hats, the extreme fashion of the well-to-do.[45]

Although Addams's words had great currency in the settlement-house movement, they were not universally embraced by other public and private agencies. Unlike the teachers,

Above: Young working women made hat-trimming an exuberant art form. Left: Cousins Sarah and Bella Weinberg dressed in their finest for this portrait in about 1915.

social workers, and college students who lived in the ethnic neighborhoods they served, other reformers tried to preserve the "American way of life" from a distance. From that perspective, the untidy pluralism of the ghetto population appeared stubbornly foreign; success could only be achieved when immigrants embraced anglicized norms. Whereas Hull-House workers valued the unique gifts and special circumstances of the immigrants, more socially conservative reformers viewed the differences as threatening, and their preachings carry the "imperious demands for conformity."[46]

With the goal of cultural assimilation rather than cultural pluralism, some middle-class observers cast a disparaging eye on the flamboyant ensembles favored by some immigrant women. While the majority of working girls, regardless of ethnic origin, favored exuberant styles of dress, some observers contrasted "the young working Jewess" for her love of finery with her frugal Italian counterpart who "was satisfied with simple fabrics."[47] Ignoring the talismanic importance of dress to the immigrant community, critics admonished working girls not to spend all of their hard-earned money on clothing. Social worker Viola Paradise, for example, felt that the Jewish girl's yearnings to look "stylish" created a set of false standards that "quite frequently express themselves in vulgarity of dress." In Paradise's opinion, the expensive tastes and inflated desires of the working girl could lead to disastrous consequences. "When the girl realizes that she will never be able to afford as many and as nice clothes as she wants . . . she is in danger of taking a wrong path to the luxuries which America has taught her to crave."[48]

Dressed in shirtwaists and tailored skirts for work, working-class women put on what

Young working women used dress to assert a sense of independence and fun.

Dorothy Richardson described as their "Cinderella clothes," for dances, parties, and the street promenade.[49] The loud colors, flashy jewelry, and flamboyant embellishments won the approval of peers but aroused the reprobation of reformers. Focusing on what they perceived as serious lack of taste, social workers extolled the virtues of restrained and simple styles. Their rhetoric suggests a link between social and sartorial control. How could they hope to Americanize women whose very clothing was a statement of insurgency? At a time when women were held to rigid behavior standards, such assertiveness and lack of social reserve could have worrisome consequences.

With "domestication" as their goal, reformers defined success in terms of a Victorian model of gracious femininity. Looking over the crowd at a University Settlement

function in New York City, a worker marveled at the settlement's success. Pointing out a well-dressed young woman, he reminisced, "I remember her when she brought her pennies to our little bank, her clothes in rags and an old shawl on her head." Transformed, these immigrants now served "the little afternoon tea," followed the American order of dinner courses, and "completely veiled [themselves] with American customs and clothing as to escape notice." [50]

But anonymity was not what most young Jewish women wanted. A noticeably changed appearance was an immediate way to signal a changing identity, and a girl's experiences with peers reinforced the importance of dressing up. Although criticized for their temerity in breaking fashion rules, many immigrant girls seemed to delight in their transgressions. They dressed for themselves and their peers, and they willfully challenged conventional notions of genteel femininity. Asserting their cultural agency, working-class young women actively created their own standards of dress.

The concept of understated "good" clothes, which reformers worked so hard to promote, collided with the immigrant's deep, and sometimes desperate, need to show off. And the frivolous, ephemeral nature of a few choice articles of dress provided welcome relief from the tedium of their everyday lives.[51] These girls daily submitted to the grinding rhythms of a factory clock; it is no wonder that they used clothing to assert a sense of individuality, independence, and fun.

How much did these young girls rebel against the dress codes of genteel America? Quite a lot, according to the Jewish press. Yiddish newspapers, magazines, and etiquette manuals reveal that many Jewish women did choose flamboyance over restraint. These publications are filled with damning examples of stylish excess. Authors admonished immigrant women in exercised tones to ape the standards of genteel society. Perhaps fearful that stylish excesses would be labeled as "too Jewish" and reflect badly on the rest of the group, the press urged restraint. Loud color combinations and gaudy ribbons hardly seem worthy of such attention, and in some instances, such venom. For hopeful aspirants, however, even the smallest social infraction could not be tolerated.

The Jewish press did more than document violations against proper etiquette and appearance; the commentary is as much prescriptive as descriptive. These working-class publications sought to validate the importance of a strong ethnic identity and, at the same time, help "their readers move toward mainstream, middle-class American life."[52] Implicitly through its selection of material and explicitly through the counsel it offered, the Jewish press advised its readers on proper dress and demeanor.

But for those immigrants who had lived a life of cultural insularity or heart-wrenching poverty in Eastern Europe, the bourgeois standards of middle-class America left them in a state of cultural shock. Many Jews remarked that America was a *farkerte velt*, an upside-down world where a "mister becomes a *shister* [shoemaker] and a *shister* a mister."[53] Young Jewish girls often felt at a distinct disadvantage because their parents were at as much of a loss as they were. Who would serve as their role models? One woman described her dilemma: "Because I came from the other side I had to work harder to become American. But my growing up didn't do me any good, because I had nobody to learn from."[54] The pervasive spirit of American individualism, which glorified the notion of personal growth, was surely as confusing as it was exciting. Bedazzled by the possibility of transcending their impoverished circumstances, émigrés still had to deal with the daily challenges of tenement life. The Old World values could be freely challenged in America, but what would take their place? For

Opposite: Chicago's Maxwell Street.

Opposite: This woman
and her daughter
perform the Rosh
Hashanah ritual of
Tashlich. The Jewish
Daily News urged
immigrant women to
observe the Sabbath
and holidays.

some immigrants, Yiddish etiquette manuals provided the answer with their promise to help the newcomers make sense of the world to which they did not yet belong.

These guides fulfilled a basic need for readers searching for social acceptance. Written specifically for the immigrant community, etiquette books covered every possible situation that might confront and confuse the newcomers. They are treatises of propriety and paeans to conformity. In his book *Etikete* (*Etiquette*), Tashrak enumerated the complicated rules of civility that would make the immigrants appear "less Polish and more polished."[55] His guide to "proper behavior, courtesy and good manners" embraces such disparate issues as card playing, flirting, table manners, and love at first sight. Jews could discover the rules of etiquette as defined by the Talmud, George Washington, and Lord Chesterfield or learn how to behave at the theater, vacation resort, or a Reform synagogue. *Etikete* is socialization at the grass-roots level.

Tashrak emphatically states that "men are better off" because they do not feel "the heavy burden that style places on" women. Acknowledging that fashion dictates constant change, he addresses the all-consuming feminine struggle to stay *au courant*; before a woman wears a new dress several times, "it is already dated." His complaint is not that Jewish women dress up, it is that they do it so badly. He urges readers to "look at the bright, shouting colors that one sees on the Jewish streets on the Sabbath or holidays. Someone with a little taste has to shudder to see how girls and young matrons . . . blindly follow new styles." Instead of following the principle that "taste comes first and style follows," the author asserts that most Jewish women have only to see a new style and "they have to grab it immediately."[56]

He tried to impress upon his audience the critical distinction between the crass parroting of American fashions on the one hand, and "real American" sophistication on the other.[57]

Color coordination, simple styles, comfortable fit, and following the rules—these were the keys to a harmonious appearance. Tashrak urged women to dress according to their age and body type: avoid furs if you weigh over two hundred pounds, stay away from checkered fabrics if you are short, and resist the temptation to battle the signs of aging with hair dyes.[58]

Not all etiquette writers gave such imperious advice. H. Malits, the author of *Di Heym un di Froy* (*The Home and the Woman*), offers an unusually sensitive perspective on the special pressures that immigrant women faced when they considered their wardrobe. Sympathizing with the poor working girl who has to dress up for her job, Malits asserts, "When you go to work you need to be properly dressed and not slovenly. But this costs money which doesn't come easily." Accounts by immigrant women confirm Malits observations. Reporting on employment in a New York department store, one salesgirl wrote that girls seeking a job in even the lowest work in any department store must wear clothing that is "at least decent looking or they won't be taken in."[59] Malits also underscored the importance of clothing to getting ahead in America. Not only is a poorly dressed girl in danger of losing her job, she is less likely to be respected. Admitting that this may or may not be just, the author accepts it as a fact of American life, and encourages his readers to do the same. He also exhorts observers to refrain from condemning working girls for spending money on themselves instead of their families. If she does not dress well, she loses the opportunity for steady employment and the "chance to marry a fine young man and to lead a life without . . . worries and anxieties."[60]

In 1913 *Di Froyen-Velt* published its inaugural issue, offering women another view of their changing world. Directed at wives and mothers who worked "at home and in the kitchen," the magazine outlined its goals in the first issue:

סטיילס און פעשיאנס

סעמי פרינצעס דרעם.

פאר קליינע פרויען און מיידלאך פון 16 ביז
18 יאהר.

מיט קורצע אדער לאנגע סליוום; רונדען אדער
הויכען קאלער; אפען אדער פארמאכט אין
פראנט סקוירט.

7985 Semi-Princesse Dress for Misses
and Small Women, 16 and 18 years.

פעטערן נומער 7985.

דיעזער פעטערן איז געשניטען אין סייזעס פאר
סטיילדאך פון 16 ביז 18 יאהר.

פאר א 16 יאהר סייז פאדערט מען וואארע, 3 יארד
27 אינטש ברייט פאר די בלאוז און פעלפום,
מיט א ½ יארד טאקס פאר'ן סענטער פראנט, און
⅞ יארד סקוירט — 18 אינטש ברייט פאר יאק. — פאר
די סקוירט — 2¼ יארד עני ברייט, די ברייט פון
סקוירט אונטען — 1½ יארד.

אום צו קריגען דיעזען פעטערן, שיקט מען אריין אין
אפיס פון „פרויען וועלט" 10 סענט און וואס פיר א סייז איהר
ווילם.

פענסי בלאוז מיט א טוניק.

מיט אדער אהן א שעמיזעט.
עס קען געטראגען ווערען אויו פיעדע סקוירט.

7967 Fancy Blouse with Tunic,
34 to 42 bust.

פעטערן נומער 7967.

דיעזער פעטערן איז געשניטען אין סייזעס פון
34 ביז 42 באסט מעזשור.

פאר א מיטעל סייז פאדערט וואארע פאר די
בלאוז, 3½ יארד — 27 אינטש ברייט, מיט 1½
יארד — 18 אינטש ברייט, פאר באנד, 7
אינטש ברייט, און ½ יארד 44 אינטש ברייט פאר
די שעמיזעט.

אום צו קריגען דיעזען פעטערן, שיקט מען אריין אין
אפיס פון „פרויען וועלט" 10 סענט און וואס פיר א סייז איהר
ווילם.

פערגעסט ניט

צו זאגען אייער ניוס-דיעלער ער זאל אייך
ברענגען דעם נעקסטען נומער
„די פרויען וועלט"

---

1 פיעס אייפראן.

צוזאמען מיט א דאסט-קעפ און האלבע סליוום.

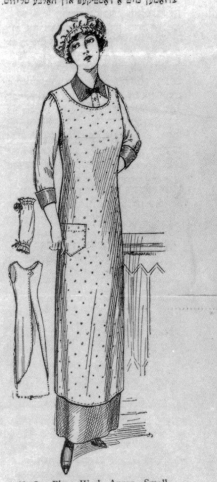

7968 One-Piece Work Apron, Small
34 or 36, Medium 38 or 40, Large 42
or 44 bust.

פעטערן נומער 7968.

דיעזער פעטערן איז געשניטען אין סייזעס פון
34 ביז 44 באסם.

פאר א מיטעל סייז, פאדערט מען וואארע 4½ יארד
27 — אינטש ברייט.

אום צו קריגען דיעזען פעטערן, שיקט מען אריין אין
אפיס פון „פרויען וועלט" 10 סענט און ניט אן
דעם נומער פון פעטערן און וואס פיר א סייז איהר
ווילט.

ערצעהלונגען

אברהם רייזען

פרייז 50 סענט.

א פראכט אויסגאבע פון 200 זייטען. ענט-
האלם סקיצעצען און בילדער וואס דער גרויסער
שרייבער און דיכטער האט געשאפען פאר דער
לעצטער צייט.

Opposite: Di Froyen-Velt *offered dress patterns that were practical in style.*

To raise the spiritual development of the Jewish woman; to help in her physical development; to familiarize her with art and literature; how to behave at home and to raise children; to deal with issues having to do with the kitchen.[61]

Throughout its brief run of a year and a half, the journal engaged Jewish women in the dialogue of Americanization. The editors offered guidance for the immigrant "anxious to learn what America means" and promised to acquaint immigrants "with the spirit of American institutions."[62] Acknowledging the challenge of merging a strong ethnic heritage with American values, it encouraged Jews to follow a pattern of assimilation that did not sunder all ties to their cultural inheritance. *Di Froyen-Velt* was outspoken on the effects of migration on the family and equally adamant about the solution: strong women who create a home of domestic stability. Tenement life, child labor, and the "spiritual emptiness of the shop" were just three of many dangers confronting the immigrants. How, one author asked, can a girl who grows up with "paint and powder," singing street songs, and reading "trashy romance novels" properly raise the next generation of Jewish children? The journal pleaded with mothers to prepare their daughters to take on the "heroic struggles" of "modern" women by inculcating them with an understanding of their Jewishness.[63]

The magazine also addressed the failure of some Jews to correctly interpret American values. In a letter to the editor, a "Jewish Gal in Rockaway" complained about the wildness of girls who, "confused with all the freedom here" after enduring the oppression of the Old World, fail to grasp the "true spirit of America." Criticizing their "vulgar" behavior and "bepowdered" appearance, the author wonders why they cannot just sit quietly and observe the ocean.[64]

But *Di Froyen-Velt* was more than a moralistic tract or a political organ. It was a magazine by women for women, and in keeping with the interests of its readers, it promoted certain kinds of fashion. Recognizing that Jewish women "look for all the opportunities to be as 'up-to-date' as non-Jewish women," the journal instructed women in "what's pretty and what is not."[65] Carefully editing out extreme styles, articles showcased fashions that they deemed morally responsible and aesthetically pleasing. With a strongly didactic voice, *Di Froyen-Velt* remained firm in its conviction that all women should strive for a conservative appearance. The magazine also provided a platform for editors to rail against the evils of paint and powder, immodest designs, and physically restrictive fashions. For example, the magazine denounced the hazardous consequences of hobble skirts and high-heeled shoes and labeled the slit skirt as "distasteful, with so little charm and so unaesthetic that it bothers anyone with any taste."[66] One particularly damning article sounded more like a battle cry than fashion rhetoric. Women were told to reject slit skirts and "free themselves not only from the oppression of men, but . . . from fashion and the sense that [they] must draw [men's] attention . . . through any means."[67]

The journal offered alternatives for its working-class readers. Women could order reasonably priced patterns of practical styles that were "very easy to make" directly through the magazine. Each issue typically featured four to six illustrated styles, complete with description and suggested fabrics. The fashions certainly never rivaled Parisian styles nor did they satisfy younger women's longings for stylish razzle-dazzle; these generic styles, however, which were tailored to meet the budgets and circumstances of an older readership, helped to initiate Jewish immigrants into their material surroundings.

The *Jewish Daily News* echoed the advice of so many reformers with its repeated assertions that simple styles, inner grace, and sensible grooming were the foundations of a pleasing

Hobble skirts were so named because their narrow hemlines prevented women from taking normal steps.

appearance. Answering the question, "What should working women wear at work?" the newspaper stressed practical concerns. While assuring readers that "I think Sarah way down on the East side has as much right to the daintiness of dress as Ida on Madison Avenue," the author of one article conceded that working women must leave some of their "pretties" at home. Dark inconspicuous colors, minimal jewelry, and serviceable shirtwaists and skirts made more sense in the workplace than feather boas and fashionable confections in delicate fabrics.[68]

The paper denounced the foolish women who carried their love of finery to fashionable extremes. There was the Kangaroo Girl, who deliberately crippled herself with narrow skirts, three-inch high heels, and a stiff high collar, as well as the thousands of girls on the East Side who ruined their eyes trying to peer through spotted face veils.[69] One columnist, the "Observer," accused these misguided fashion

plates of deliberately "turning on the screw of torture," out of a misplaced love of style rather than beauty.[70] And what of the girl whose "sweet temper turns sour" from high-heeled shoes and tight corsets, and who spends money she can ill afford on gaudy robes and gay hats just because of fashion? According to the Observer, "she follows the crowd, but leaves character behind."[71] The columnist turned a baleful eye on the "Ghetto girl" who has carried her "evolution" to the point where she is "dying from improvement."[72] But the writer leveled the harshest criticism against the "wanton Jews" who satisfied their consumer cravings on holy days. These offenders, including "girls, who, by their appearance, indicate a most recent arrival from Poland or Galicia," shopped on the Sabbath, thereby desecrating the day with their search for bargains.

The list of infractions went on. In her "Just Between Ourselves, Girls" column, "Zelda" accused young girls of selfishly buying "silken rags" with their earnings, money that could be used to clothe, feed, and keep the rest of her family warm. Drawing an image worthy of Dickens, she admonished: "You fill your trunk with silk and lisle-thread hose, while your own little sisters and brothers . . . get their little feet blistered from the stockings that have been a dozen times patched and mended."[73] The columnist praised a modest appearance, good grooming, and a "careful toilet." But even this goal held potential risks—if a girl became too neat, she turned into a "Fussy Fanny" who will "work on your nerves." Constantly worrying and "hyper-neat," Fussy was always in motion, fidgeting, adjusting, and bombarding companions with endless questions. "Is my hat on straight? How does this veil look? Is my hair up nicely this evening?" No wonder Zelda wanted to run in the other direction!

One can only imagine a young woman's sighs of exasperation over such curmudgeonly advice. But immigrant women found more than disparagement in the Yiddish press. Some writers praised the efforts of Jewish East Siders, frequently singling out a well-dressed crowd at a social event. In 1897, the "Doctor's Column," which was devoted to the interests of the "younger element," refuted the claims that Jewish girls do not know how to dress:

> Some of our girls, of course, dress more tastefully than others, but as a whole they are fully as well dressed as any other girls in this town. They do it pretty cheaply, too!. . . . They have that knack of making a most attractive gown out of popular-priced goods. This is quite an accomplishment.[74]

Occasionally the *Jewish Daily News* devoted a column to the newest colors and latest styles. In 1898, for example, readers learned about the popularity of "dainty hammock dresses" of flowered muslin, the "picturesque" charm of a Marie Antoinette fichu (collar), and the growing popularity of that "blatant hue," cock's-comb red.[75] This same paper that moralized against artifice, however, carried advertisements that sent a very different message. The *Tageblatt* noted in February 1900, for example, that "to look beautiful is a duty which the fair sex owes both to themselves and their friends." With regular application of Dr. Gouraud's Magical Beautifier, even freckled, "pimpled or moth-patched" skin could be made "like the new-born babes."[76]

Etiquette writers, social workers, landsleit, educators—so many "experts" were just waiting to help the newcomers become less green and more American. Promising success, these cultural arbiters bombarded immigrants with advice. But did the newcomers pay attention? Like so many historical polemics, the answer is layered in complexities. The Jews who left Eastern Europe at the turn of the century were not a unified culture. They formed a vibrant mixture of people with varied backgrounds, different interpretations of their faith, and a plurality of experiences; their responses to Americanization were equally diverse. While Sara Abrams loved to attend classes at a settlement house, her parents "shunned all the institutions that offered . . . aid to the foreigner."[77] One girl, who came to this country at age fifteen, blamed her parent's foreign ways for her own lack of assimilation.[78] Yet Ella Wolf, who emigrated at the same age, felt "as if I were born here."[79] Some women seized every opportunity to embrace a new culture and a new identity while others felt trapped in a painful state of limbo. One of Anzia Yezierska's heroines observes: "I can't live with the old world, and I'm yet too green for the new."[80]

As historian Roy Rosenzweig points out, "Cultures do not change overnight or even over fifty years."[81] Yet faced with the disreputable status of greenhorn, emigrants needed some immediate reassurance that their splintered self-image could be renovated. For the vast majority of newcomers, clothing provided that reassurance. Even if they received conflicting messages about the form fashion should take, there was unanimous agreement about its function. Sociologists debate whether dress can trigger any kind of lasting or meaningful change in a person's identity, but that debate belongs to the classroom. For millions of Jewish immigrants and their counselors of consumption, it was true.

Notes

1. Elisabeth Howe Bliss, "Intimate Studies in the Lives of Fifty Working Girls," (master's thesis, Columbia University, 1915), 83.

2. Sara J. Abrams, "Nothing is Not Anything," American Jewish Autobiographies, YIVO Archives, YIVO Institute for Jewish Research.

3. Rose Krawetz, Ellis Island Oral History Project, Ellis Island Immigration Museum.

4. Nahma Sandrow, "Yiddish Theater and American Theater," in Sarah Blacher Cohen, ed., *From Hester Street to Hollywood: The Jewish-American Stage and Screen* (Bloomington, Ind.: 1986), 22.

5. Maxine Schwartz Seller, *To Seek America: A History of Ethnic Life in the United States* (Englewood, N.J.: 1988), 176–77.

6. Sydelle Kramer and Jenny Masur, eds., *Jewish Grandmothers* (Boston: 1976), 145.

7. Max and Milton Shatsky, Ellis Island Oral History Project.

8. Celia Adler, Ellis Island Oral History Project.

9. "Minnie Publicker Interview," American Jewish Archives, Cincinnati Campus, Hebrew Union College, Jewish Institute of Religion.

10. Kramer and Masur, *Jewish Grandmothers*, 27.

11. Fannie Friedman, Ellis Island Oral History Project.

12. Ivan Chermayeff, Fred Wasserman, and Mary J. Shapiro, *Ellis Island: An Illustrated History of the Immigrant Experience* (New York: 1991), 26.

13. "LKF Writings/Manuscript Notes," Ludmila K. Foxlee Papers, Box 1, Folder 11, Ellis Island Archives.

14. "LKF Personal/Writings," Ludmila K. Foxlee Papers, Box 1, Folder 17, Ellis Island Archives.

15. "LKF Writings/Manuscript Notes," Ludmila K. Foxlee Papers, Box 1, Folder 11, Ellis Island Archives.

16. Ludmila K. Foxlee, "How They Came: The Drama of Ellis Island 1920–1935," unpublished manuscript, 1968, 135, 195, Ellis Island Archives.

17. *New York Tribune*, August 16, 1903; reprinted in Allon Schoener, ed., *Portal to America: The Lower East Side 1870–1925* (New York: 1967), 105.

18. Faina Burko, "The American Yiddish Theater and Its Audience Before World War I," in David Berger, ed., *The Legacy of Jewish Migration: 1881 and Its Impact* (New York: 1983), 92–93.

19. Mary Antin, *The Promised Land* (Boston: 1912), 72.

20. Antin, *The Promised Land*, 246–47.

21. Andrew R. Heinze, *Adapting to Abundance: Jewish Immigrants, Mass Consumption, and the Search for American Identity* (New York: 1990), 89.

22. Jennie Schaffner, interview with Eden Rosenbush, June 19, 1993.

23. Edward Steiner, "The Russian and Polish Jew in New York," *Outlook*, November 1, 1902, 503.

24. Horace M. Kallen, "Democracy Versus the Melting-Pot: A Study of American Nationality," *Nation*, February 19, 1915, 192.

25. Hutchins Hapgood, *The Spirit of the Ghetto* (New York: 1902); reprinted with introduction by Moses Rischin (Cambridge: 1967), 71.

26. Elizabeth Ewen, *Immigrant Women in the Land of Dollars: Life and Culture on the Lower East Side, 1890–1925* (New York: 1985), 162–63.

27. Anna Kuthan Oral History, Immigrant Labor History Project.

28. Max Grossman, Ellis Island Oral History Project.

29. Idisore Witsotsky, "Such a Life," American Jewish Autobiographies, #288, YIVO Archives, YIVO Institute for Jewish Research.

30. Lucy Robins Lang, *Tomorrow is Beautiful* (New York: 1948), 15.

31. Lillian Gorenstein, "A Memoir of the Great War, 1914–1924 (In memory of my beloved brother, Morris)," YIVO Archives, vol. 20: 172–73.

32. Sara J. Abrams, "Things Trivial," American Jewish Autobiographies, #92, YIVO Archives.

33. Ida Richter, Tape I, Papers of Jenny Masur, YIVO Archives.

34. Mario Puzo, *The Fortunate Pilgrim* (New York: 1964), 10.

35. Kramer and Masur, *Jewish Grandmothers*, 85.

36. "Jennie Matyas and the I.L.G.W.U.," interview with Jennie Matyas by Corinne Gilb, 12, Industrial Relations Library, University of California, Berkeley.

37. Simon Patten, *The Consumption of Wealth* (New York: 1892), 51.

38. Gunther Barth, *City People: The Rise of Modern City Culture in Nineteenth Century America* (New York: 1980), 129.

39. Heinze, *Adapting to Abundance*, 10.

40. Ella Wolf, Oral History Collection, YIVO Archives.

41. Rose Harriet Pastor, "Millinery Row," *Jewish Daily News*, June 11, 1903.

42. Mina K. Friedman, "Time About No News To All," unpublished manuscript, courtesy of Alan Friedman.

43. Ellen Richardson, *The Woman Who Spends* (Boston: 1913), 77–78.

44. Jane Addams, "The Subtle Problems of Charity," *Atlantic Monthly*, February 1899, 168.

45. Addams, "The Subtle Problems of Charity," 169.

46. Robert A. Carlson, "Americanization as an Early Twentieth-Century Adult Education Movement," *History of Education Quarterly*, 20:4 (Winter 1970).

47. Rudolf Glanz, *The Jewish Woman in America: Two Female Immigrant Generations 1820–1928*, vol. I: The Eastern European Jewish Woman (New York: 1976), 87.

48. Viola Paradise, "The Jewish Immigrant Girl in Chicago," *Survey*, September 6, 1913, 704.

49. Dorothy Richardson, *The Long Day: The Story of a Working Girl as Told by Herself* (New York: 1905), 95.

50. "The Jewish Quarter of Harlem," *The Jewish Daily News*, February 23, 1904.

51. Kathy Peiss, *Cheap Amusements: Working Women and Leisure in Turn-of-the-Century New York* (Philadelphia: 1986), 66–67.

52. Maxine Seller, "The World of Our Mothers: The Woman's Page of the Jewish Daily Forward," *Journal of Ethnic Studies,* 16(2) (Summer 1988): 96.

53. Heinze, *Adapting to Abundance,* 97.

54. Sydney Stahl Weinberg, *The World of Our Mothers: The Lives of Jewish Immigrant Women* (Chapel Hill: 1988), 103.

55. Tashrak with the assistance of A. Tanenboym, D. M. Hermalin, and others, *Etikete* (New York: 1912).

56. Tashrak, *Etikete,* 41–64.

57. Eli Lederhendler, "Guides for the Perplexed: Sex, Manners, and Mores for the Yiddish Reader in America," unpublished manuscript.

58. Tashrak, *Etikete,* 41–64.

59. "A Salesgirl's Story," in Leon Stern and Philip Taft, eds., *Workers Speak, Self Portraits* (New York: 1971), 3.

60. H. Malits, *Di Heym un di Froy* (New York: 1918), 166–70.

61. *Di Froyen-Velt*, April 13, 1913, 5.

62. *Di Froyen-Velt*, April 13, 1913, 1.

63. "Our Daughters," *Di Froyen-Velt*, May 1913, 1–4.

64. "Letter to the Editor," *Di Froyen-Velt*, July 1915, 18–19.

65. "The Latest Fashions in Women's Clothing," *Di Froyen-Velt*, September 1913, 3.

66. "From the Woman's World," *Di Froyen-Velt*, September 1913, 10; "The Latest Fashions in Women's Clothing," *Di Froyen-Velt*, September 1913, 4.

67. "The Latest Fashions in Women's Clothing," *Di Froyen-Velt*, 1.

68. "Advice to Working Women," *Jewish Daily News*, December 2, 1898.

69. "Just Between Ourselves, Girls," *Jewish Daily News*, December 27, 1903.

70. "The Stylish Face-Veil." *Jewish Daily News*, June 24, 1904.

71. "Following the Merry Crowd," *Jewish Daily News*, December 29, 1904.

72. "Chapeaux Bas!" *Jewish Daily News*, February 23, 1900.

73. "Just Between Ourselves, Girls," *Jewish Daily News*, December 22, 1903.

74. "The Doctor's Column," *Jewish Daily News*, October 1, 1897.

75. "The Fashions," *Jewish Daily News*, August 31, 1898.

76. *Yiddish Tageblatt*, February 16, 1900.

77. Abrams, "Nothing is Not Anything."

78. Sydney Stahl Weinberg, "Jewish Mothers and Immigrants Daughters: Positive and Negative Role Models," *Journal of American Ethnic History*, 6(2) (Spring 1987): 39–40.

79. Ella Wolf, Oral History Collection, YIVO Archives.

80. Anzia Yezierska, *Children of Loneliness* (New York: 1923), 122.

81. Roy Rosenzweig, *Eight Hours For What We Will: Workers & Leisure in an Industrial City, 1870–1920* (Cambridge: 1983), 215.

Mothers and Daughters

The diverse historical situation of Jews in the Old World and the wide constellation of influences they encountered in the New World argues against any homogenization of the immigrant experience.[1] Yet it is certain women experienced the move differently than men did. Acting as the domestic caretaker and emotional connector, women labored to keep their families together in unimaginable circumstances. In the Old Country, mothers protected their family from a world of poverty, oppression, and dislocation. Many men migrated earlier to make a home and enough money for steamship tickets, so women often found themselves struggling alone. Other families sent their oldest children, including their working-age daughters, to live with friends or relatives. They worked to pave the way for the rest of the family, while their mothers worried at home.[2] Once they reached America, mothers faced the daily ordeal of resettlement. An article that appeared in *Di Froyen-Velt* captured the painful consequences of this historical dislocation. "We gave up a life we were accustomed to. In our middle age, sometimes older, we have to start a new life. We are as if newborn when we come to America."[3] Thrust into an alien environment with more hope than money, a Jewish woman was expected to be the family's protector, financial custodian, and stabilizing center; her own needs hung somewhere in the balance.

Not only did married women have to find their way in new surroundings without the cultural, religious, and family supports of their homeland, but they had to cope with children raised in a foreign environment. In their desire to become "American," many younger immigrants embraced new codes of behavior and appearance that challenged the dominance of parental authority. As they established themselves in urban, industrialized settings, daughters questioned the relevance of their mothers' Old World customs. And through their questioning, they jeopardized immigrant mothers' dominance as viable role models. The hurt that Jewish mothers felt over such rejection was more than a personal disappointment; they feared the unraveling of their cultural universe.[4] Viewed through the youthful prism of modernity, the religious values of the shtetl seemed old-fashioned. America rewarded winners, and immigrants who wanted to succeed had to devote themselves to "the secular deities of money and work."[5]

Opposite: Sarah Maremont and her daughter Agatha.

Right: Young women who worked outside of the home faced a different set of challenges than did their mothers.

121

Immigrant women could not help but feel vulnerable as they confronted the unfamiliar and struggled to deal with the pangs of separation. One contemporary observer noted that "perhaps at no time of her adult life is the immigrant girl more impressionable . . . than during her first few months in America. . . . American life can mold her as it will."[6] We must take into consideration that these words come from a social reformer intent on conversion, yet her rhetoric contains an important truth. Arrival in America brought with it a heightened sense of self-consciousness as the newcomers tried to etch an identity. They had to ask questions that were as much moral choices as lifestyle judgments. "How much of the New World should I embrace?" "How much of the Old World should I preserve?" "What choices will my children make?"

Mothers, safe from the physical peril and blatant discrimination that threatened their families in Eastern Europe, could begin to hope for a better life, and they centered their hopes on their children. To Fannie Shoock's mother, America offered the unthinkable: an education for her daughters. Delightedly, she would say: "It's the most wonderful thing in America that your child can go to school with Gentile children, come home, her hair isn't torn, her dress isn't torn, she isn't beaten up."[7] Other women took great pride in their children's American ways. As the youngest girl in a large family, one Russian immigrant received all of her education in America while her older sister had to go to work. "My parents were very proud of me because I was *di Amerikaneh* (the American)."[8] When the tempo of modern city life left some mothers breathless, they encouraged their sons and daughters to act as intermediaries between the public and private worlds. Dr. Morris Moel remembered that his mother:

> had to learn how to cook a little differently because we as children going to school, learned a little about what we were supposed

Above: School graduations were important milestones for many immigrant parents who dreamed of an education for their children. Left: Fay Kanter's diploma from Oliver Goldsmith School.

Opposite: Surrounded by her fashionable daughters Dora Ruben, seated at left, wore a kerchief and simple dress.

to eat, how we're supposed to dress and those things were a reflection to her from our experiences in school.[9]

But women discovered that the promise of the New World contained risks as well as opportunities. As children broadened their cultural horizons, they moved beyond the orbit of parental authority. In the process, generations became divided by an emotional wedge. In her 1904 study of East Side Jews, Belle Mead discussed the problems created by different patterns of assimilation: "The old women, still wearing the law-proscribed wigs, watch their children in the public schools make rapid strides . . . while they, in the eyes of these very

Opposite: Older immigrant women often stayed within their immediate neighborhood where they were surrounded by familiar faces, customs, and language.

Right: Rochel Leah Wagman and her children. Rochel (front center) wore a sheitel while her Americanized daughters chose the fashionable bob.

children, still remain foreigners or 'greenies.'"[10] Lena, a young garment worker, felt only scorn as she looked at her mother across the generational divide. She was a "greenhorn," and thus "inferior to me, an Americanized girl."[11]

Trying to uphold the traditions of her homeland, the Old World mother had to contend with her American children's religious neglect. While the mother still exerted a voice of authority and received obedience, her daughter's "inward life, experiences and trials are lived apart. . . . In Jewish homes religion is with the parents and it remains there."[12] Settlement-house worker Lillian Wald observed that the modern world of America was particularly threatening to Orthodox Jews, who found themselves "without anchor."[13] Mothers who relied on Old World customs to provide a sense of continuity watched with bewilderment as

their children adopted untraditional behavior and appearance. J. Pfeffer wrote in 1902 that as young people plunge into big city life, parents "find themselves a hundred years behind time." He presents a dramatic image of the cultural chasm:

> At the time when the Jewish mother stands, inspired, by her Sabbath candles listening to the benediction of her husband, her daughters are in the parlor with young men, playing the piano and entertaining themselves in many other sacrilegious ways.[14]

Such differences could not help but create enormous dissension. In this contest between the sacred and the secular, we glimpse the full impact of immigration on Jewish families.

Watching their children's rapid assimilation, many mothers felt left behind. In her story, "Fat of the Land," Anzia Yezierska exposed the accumulated tensions between generations. Aspiring to the life of an American "lady," Fanny finds little to admire or emulate in her own mother. She complains:

> God knows how hard I tried to civilize her so as not to have to blush with shame when I take her anywhere. I dressed in the most stylish Paris models, but Delancy Street sticks out from every inch of her. Whenever she opens her mouth, I'm done for.[15]

While the immigrant voices recorded in oral histories are rarely this strident or critical, they do make it clear that in many families, mothers and daughters lived in very different worlds. Trying to maintain some equilibrium in the midst of tremendous upheaval, many older women confined their world to their home and neighborhood. Insecure with their newly acquired identity and often too burdened to learn English, they deliberately narrowed their locus of activity. The animated collage of city life sometimes seemed threatening, particularly with the memories of pogroms and destruction still fresh in their consciousness. Estelle Belford remembers her father reassuring her mother that, finally, she was safe. Urging her to go out in the street and mingle with people, he said, "You're in America now and you have nothing to be afraid of. Nothing at all."[16]

Immigrants who felt overwhelmed by their radically new environment found solace in the familiarity of their neighborhood. Protected from the chaos of urbanization, Jewish mothers asserted their control through the fixed rituals of their culture. In these ethnic enclaves, surrounded by relatives and bound by a common language and customs, Jewish women could purchase kosher food, celebrate holidays, and "exchange news of the homeland."[17] Bound together by shared hardships, women who might have been separated by class in Eastern Europe came together in America for support.[18]

But the younger generation sorely felt the limitations of this homebound existence. An evening in the parlor under a parent's watchful eye could hardly compete with the beckoning excitement of dance halls, amusement parks, or nickelodeons. While they still depended on what Irving Howe aptly refers to as the "social padding" of the immigrant community, adolescent girls were willing to venture beyond the few blocks that narrowly defined their parents' home.[19] Their exposure to an urbanized world created a longing for new experiences, an appetite whetted by America's promise and encouraged by peers. They wanted to spend time with each other and with men.

When parents accused the younger generation of rebellion, their daughters uttered the time-worn complaint: "You just don't understand!" Treated as independent adults at work during the day, some daughters chafed at the parental rules they encountered each evening. In 1905 the *Forward* published an article highlighting the conflict experienced by young Jewish typists:

> At work a girl . . . hears and speaks English only. Her betters treat her with respect. . . . But at home, living in dirty rooms, she's plain "Beyle" or "Khontsche." Her parents . . . pounce upon her if she expresses an interest in a new hat. If she mentions a ball, they tell her to dance with the laundry.[20]

The challenges of assimilation did not always lead to crisis: different did not have to equal dire. Simarly, immigrants' responses did not fall neatly into generational camps; this was a complex process mediated by other factors such as class, gender, and cultural background. Yet these issues rarely surface in people's memories. It is the New World clashes between parents and children that they remember. But why? Surely they bickered in the Old World, yet the retelling of these family tensions lack the emotional power of New World disagreements. Immigrants' polarized vocabulary

Amusement parks such as New York's Dreamland (above) and Chicago's Riverview (below) offered opportunities to parade one's style.

new beginning. When her husband, who had come to the United States nine years earlier, "showed her what American women looked like . . . she stopped wearing the sheitel. She wanted to be modern." After they were settled, Sally and her sisters bought their mother new clothes and took her to have her hair done "so she would look American."[21]

Some daughters also understood that while they might embrace a more modern lifestyle, there was much to value in their mothers' world. In her unpublished memoirs, Sara J. Abrams draws a portrait of her mother's "foreign" ways with great affection:

> If I could only draw a picture . . . of a woman, round of hip, and buxom of breast. . . . She would be holding a small paring knife in one hand, and a partially peeled potato in the other. . . . She would possibly be shaking her head, at the inquirer or solicitor, with the words: "I am sorrie . . . I am onli the lady in the hose."[22]

Left: Bessie Adler.

Below: Young women relied on peers rather than parents for fashion and other advice.

Opposite: Chicago's 12th Street Store advertised its affordable fashions in Yiddish newspapers.

suggests that there was more to squabble over in America. The longed-for opportunities meant that choices could be made, and these choices challenged immigrants to rethink their possibilities. Still rooted in the mutual dependence of family life, mothers and daughters also heard America's celebratory message of individualism.

Oral histories are testimony to the diversity of attitudes among Jewish immigrants, and they suggest that in many families relationships, though strained and tested, remained fundamentally supportive. In others, mothers felt the magnetic pull of fashion as strongly as their daughters, and they closed the gap between the generations by demonstrating both an eagerness and a capacity to embrace a different lifestyle. Sally Goldstein remembered that her mother, Chana, made a dramatic break with the past shortly after arriving in Chicago. Wanting to signal the end of the extreme poverty that her family endured in Russia, Chana looked for an appropriate symbol of her

And in still other families, daughters and mothers remained rooted in their Jewishness and worked together to preserve their cultural heritage.

But many households, shaken by long periods of separation and struggling with momentous changes, could not sustain the aftershocks

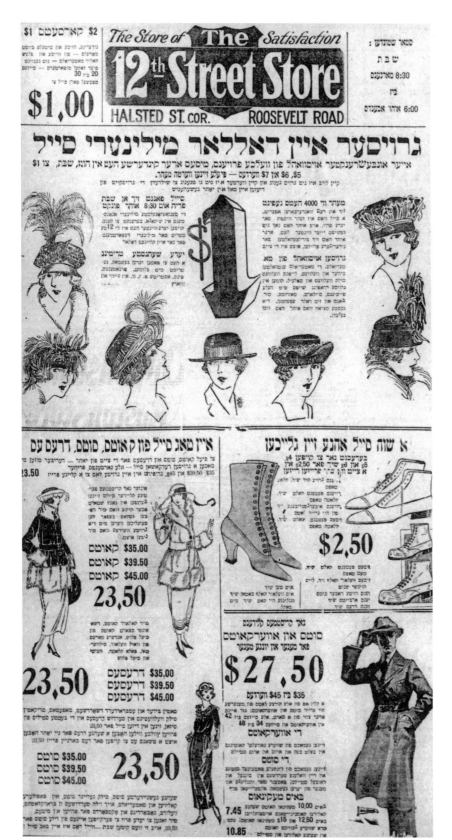

of this culture clash. Warring expectations of mothers and daughters tore at the fabric of domestic life and divided the family along generational lines. Devoutly religious women, unwilling or unable to engage in the process of "Americanization," risked censure from their children as well as from society. Daughters who learned in America to assert their individual rights began to openly challenge parental authority. One woman recalled clashing with her mother over the seemingly trivial issue of hair ribbons:

> Once mother was tying a ribbon in my hair and the bow just wouldn't come out straight. I was terribly angry and when she asked me why, I replied that *An alte mameh ken nit farbinden shain a ribben.* (An old mother cannot tie a ribbon nicely.)[23]

As differences escalated, some mothers and daughters found themselves on opposite sides of an ideological debate; progress for the younger generation translated into disintegrative social upheaval for their parents. In this battle of rival perceptions, dress became a tangible expression of alienation and an explosive source of intergenerational conflict.

After studying ninety immigrant families in Chicago, Sophonisba Breckenridge concluded that of all the issues confronting the generations, clothing was the most likely to engender conflict. "It is to be expected that the girl of foreign-born parents should quickly learn at school or at work . . . that to be well dressed is to be dressed in the latest fashion. . . . and early learns the unimportance of quality in modern clothes."[24] Mothers accustomed to purchasing clothes for their longevity found this yardstick of value particularly distressing. But fashion, by definition, implies change, prizing the ephemeral over the enduring.[25] Americanized girls knew that their peers admired stylish ensembles; attributes such as "sturdy" and "durable" would hardly merit an enthusiastic response.

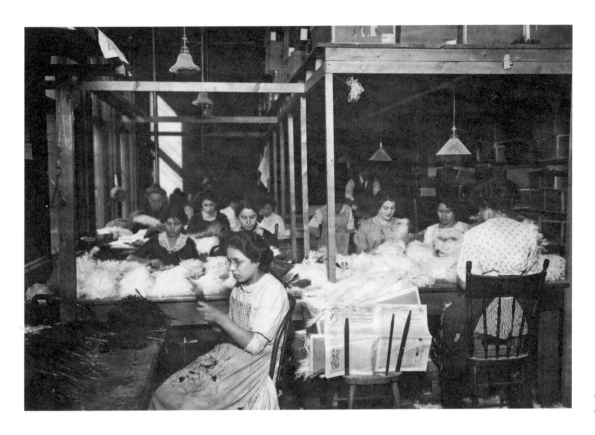

In the workplace, young women developed close friendships with their peers.

Celia Ruben and Joseph Paul courting at Chicago's Riverview Park.

Writing about her experience as a factory worker, one woman observed that "a shop girl is always sweller in her dress, no matter how poor she may be, than her relatives. Ashamed of her family, she meets young men 'on the outside' rarely taking them home."[26] Impatient with their parents' ignorance of the New World, Jewish youth looked to other sources for their role models. Sol Meyrowitz remembered his misery over the gulf between his parents who "didn't do things the way Americans did things" and his very "modern" sister:

> She used lipstick and went to burlesque shows. In those years, in our house, it was *verboten*. In those years, she went to dances and all the things that were frowned upon she went to. I don't know where she learned it—maybe from the movies.[27]

Seeking approval from fashion-wise peers not fashion-indifferent parents, some girls shifted loyalties. Gussie M. tried to put as much distance as possible between herself and her mother. "Everything that my mother did, I decided to do the opposite," she recalled.[28]

Contemporaries understood the importance of stylish clothing and introduced new arrivals to the rich lexicon of American fashion. By comparison, the scripted advice of parents seemed hopelessly out of date. When Ida Feldman arrived from Poland, her father told her that "a girl of sixteen has to go to work." Understanding that she needed new clothing, he took her to a store and purchased a second-hand outfit. But the result was far from pleasing to Ida. "I hate to tell you what I looked like with a pair of black stockings," as she went off to work stitching hems for five dollars a week.[29]

Young girls lived a more public life than their mothers; thus, they dressed for a different audience. The social world of work was a competitive arena where co-workers placed a pre-mium on appearance. As one sixteen-year-old garment worker explained: "A girl who does not dress well is stuck in a corner, even if she is pretty."[30] Another girl recalled being judged by her clothing the first day on the job. "I had on a heavy winter coat, just a plain, rough-looking coat, but it's warm." When she approached one of the workers, she was met "by such a look, a sort of sneering look—oh, it made me hot! But that's the way American shop-girls are."[31]

In his autobiography, Marcus Ravage sharply criticized the competitiveness that dominated American society. Mourning the passing of the shtetl's spirit of cooperation, he remembered a time when people handed down "solid and substantial things" from one generation to another, "not the fleeting vanities of dress."[32] But young girls determined to make America their home grew impatient with stories that began "In my day. . . ." Dazzled by the

Young people came together on lunch hours and after work.

surrounding cluster of new products and images, they seized upon fashion as a vital link to their evolving self-image. Although their clothing may have been cheap, it was up-to-the-minute in style.[33]

Rejecting the subtle appeal of sartorial understatements, Jewish girls favored brash ensembles that flaunted their fashion know-how. Ida Richter remembered sharing an admiration for American fashions with her fellow workers. "We used to love the American people, to copy them."[34] Undaunted that their meager earnings often prevented them from purchasing the very clothes they made at work, Jewish girls used their sewing skills, bargaining talents, and keen eye to assemble an American wardrobe.

Finding endless opportunities for variation and parody, immigrants were more than "queens of imitation"; they playfully adapted the looks of the rich and intentionally over-dressed to "put on style."[35] The social workers who accused female immigrants of vulgarity and decried their "pronounced lack of modesty in dress" missed the point.[36] These girls were looking for visibility. And so they sampled, mixed, and reassembled the decorative with the practical to create a range of hybrid styles with fantastic embellishments. The fashions of a "shriekingly red jacket," "crimped and frizzled hair," or "white shirtwaist funnily bestruck with magenta ribbons" might not be refined but they got a girl noticed.[37] With precious little money to spend, working girls wanted articles of dress that would parade their stylishness as conspicuously as possible. When Elizabeth Hasanovitz went to work in a shirtwaist factory, her co-workers created a dress for her out of scraps of cotton voile. "They teased me, saying, 'Now you are ready for the country—upon our words, with this dress on, you'll have all them fellows out there after you.'"[38] For the grand sum of sixty cents, she had an outfit that would provoke attention. Not all hand-fashioned outfits were as successful. Young Frieda

At the turn of the century, arranged marriages were losing favor, especially with young people. This American postcard promotes the notion of romantic love.

Young girls dressed to capture the attention of admiring young men.

remembered making a new dress when her family settled in Minneapolis. Pleased with the results, she showed off her creation to a stylish friend. "Look, Lola, I made," Frieda exclaimed. Lola looked her up and down and said "It looks like it!"[39]

Taking their cues from the larger trends and seeking the stylish badges of acceptance, working girls developed their own fashion sense; that they had to piece together outfits from disparate parts and sew their own clothing in no way weakened their purpose or pleasure. Indeed, the process enabled them to create customized fashions. Wanting more than diluted, yet affordable, versions of elite dresses, immigrant women saved their pennies, scrimped on essentials, and salvaged scraps from the cutting-room floor to create styles that met their own tastes. Their efforts help us to understand that adoption of new styles depends as much on the flow of information within groups as between them.[40] Despite the trickle-down theory, which assumes that fashions originate with the elite and move downward, working girls sought inspiration from numerous sources, finding fashion innovators in the streets and factories, as well as in mass-marketed ideals.

Jane Addams understood that the "preposterous clothing" and "huge hat with its wilderness of feathers" of young working girls were more than fashion statements. She wrote that such ensembles announced "to the world" that the girl "is here . . . ready to live."[41] Mothers who dedicated themselves to feminine ideals of modesty and to clothing principles of utility might wince at such extravagant aggression, but their pleas were often ignored. Their daughters made an intimate connection between symbols of stylishness and the immediate needs of their everyday life. Buoyed by youthful narcissism and supported by peers, shopgirls dressed in a way that proclaimed their intentions and independence.

To pay for new clothing, working girls looked for ways to save money, often skipping meals or walking to work to save the fare. Shirtwaist worker Clara Lemlich told a reporter that to buy a new hat, "even if it hasn't cost more than fifty cents, means that we have gone for weeks on two-cent lunches—dry cake and nothing else."[42] In her autobiography, factory worker Elisabeth Hasanovitz described how even the smallest of pleasures demanded sacrifice:

> If we rejoiced in one thing, we did it at the expense of another. At the expense of our sleep we went to the library; at the expense of a few dinners we went to the opera; at the expense of a better room we bought a dress; at the expense of our leisure we did our laundry.[43]

Dressing up meant sacrifice, yet the results offered great joy. At her father's insistence, Mina Friedman began working in a factory as a shirtwaist packer when she turned fourteen. Accepting her responsibility to "help out at home," Mina turned her pay envelope over to her parents. "I didn't earn much, but that didn't matter; one had to work and help out at home; you gave your money to your parents . . . and in return you got an allowance." Mina used her allowance to buy stockings, shoes, dresses, and "once, what a thrill, my first pair of white silk gloves." The cost of the gloves required several weeks of savings, but the pleasure was worth the sacrifice. "They were the real treasure of my life," said Mina.[44]

The apparent ease of Mina's arrangement, however, betrays the struggles that heightened tensions between some children and parents. In the patriarchal order of Jewish tradition, the spending of family money was a "cornerstone of parental authority."[45] Many parents, believing in an interdependent family system, expected their children to hand over their pay envelopes unopened. But some youth questioned this logic. Although they wanted to honor their family responsibilities, surely their breadwinning efforts entitled them to an allowance. In her

1915 study of fifty working girls, Elizabeth Bliss interviewed three working sisters who had varying interpretations of their filial duty. While Ada, the "practical one," turned over all of her wages and spent her evenings at home reading or sewing, Mabel, the "butterfly," wanted to keep all her money to spend on clothing or amusements. And although the middle daughter, Ruth, would hand over her unopened pay envelope during difficult times, she seemed to worry more about not having a new dress than about "the fact that the family was actually having a hard time this winter."[46]

The overwhelming majority of Jewish girls understood that their families depended on their wages to improve their lot or even just to maintain a basic level of subsistence. Eager to do their part, young girls dropped out of school and entered the work force when they were in their early teens. Buying steamship tickets, paying for a brother's education, and contributing to the monthly rent were a girl's top priorities. But earning money and developing relationships outside of the home encouraged a burgeoning sense of independence, and adolescents began to see themselves as autonomous beings in control of their own lives. Emboldened by their economic power, some girls increased their demands for discretionary income. Striving to support their families, they wanted a little bit for themselves. Work exposed girls to the world outside the family, where material matters seemed more immediate than spiritual ones. They learned that the lights of America's cities beckoned with the promise of personal fulfillment, but it came with a price tag. To participate one had to spend.[47] Determined to reap the rewards of their labor, working girls, like sixteen-year-old Sadie Frowne, wanted access to money so that they could "put on plenty of style."[48]

Generations collided over purchases as working daughters demanded spending autonomy. While mothers often understood their

Opposite: New York's Coney Island.

Mina Friedman (below) scrimped and saved for weeks to buy her first pair of white silk gloves, which she described as "the real treasure of my life."

children's desire for consumer pleasures and shared a similar longing, they had the needs of the entire family to consider. Meager household budgets and uncertain wages left women wondering how to pay for rent and put food on the table. Concerned with their families' future, financially conservative mothers pinched pennies and made daily sacrifices so that they might create some measure of security. They also quieted their own yearnings for stylish fashions. A 1909 study of working-class family budgets in New York revealed that a mother's yearly expenditure on clothing was consistently the lowest.[49] S. B. Breckenridge found that while many older women went barefoot in Chicago's Jewish neighborhoods, it was not out of a desire to preserve Old World customs. Instead, she argued, the women went barefoot to save money so that "their children may wear 'American shoes.'"[50] But unlike their frugal mothers, many young girls wanted instant gratification. When told by her mother that only working girls needed new clothing, one fourteen-year-old girl decided to quit school and get a job.[51]

Girls also wanted the independence to buy things that they valued regardless of their parents' wishes. One woman remembers her sister taking part of her weekly paycheck and buying things to wear to dances. "She was the first one to bring lipstick and other makeup into the house and my father called her a *gassen froi* (street woman)."[52] Unrepentant, the girl continued to indulge in the fashionable pleasures that made the monotony of factory work worthwhile.

Jean W.'s relationship with her mother erupted over the issue of a blouse. Jean found a blouse on Grand Street in New York City priced at three dollars, but her mother only allowed her to keep two of the eleven dollars she earned each week. Jean's mother encouraged her to purchase a simpler, cheaper style reasoning that Jean "wasn't that kind of fancy skinny Marie." But Jean stubbornly refused. If she

Above: Generations clashed over issues of spending autonomy. Left: Fannie Neymark c. 1907.

could not get that blouse, she "was not going to get a blouse at all." In defiance, Jean kept her paycheck, unopened, for four weeks. Her father finally settled the dispute with the suggestion that Jean pay one dollar a day for room and board and keep the remaining four dollars for herself. Triumphantly, Jean agreed to the arrangement and continued to spend her money as she wanted. "I used to go out on Clinton Street and get a hat for $25 . . . and my mother used to say, 'What's on this hat, gold?'"[53]

Finding resistance at home, young girls turned to each other for support. In the factories and shop rooms, peers cemented their friendships with shared confidences of beaux and clothes, reveling in tales of "romantic conquests."[54] Bella H. remembered working in the shops and "singing the dream songs, the love songs."[55] For girls like Mollie, an eighteen-year-old machine operator, marriage was the only way of moving up and out. "The girl next to me got married last week and so she escaped." Mollie promised, "That's what I am going to do some day."[56] Accepting matrimony as their desirable fate, these girls pursued a common goal—getting a fellow.

At the turn of the century, a single girl had few options. Expected to leave the protection of her father's home only to move directly into a husband's arms, adolescent girls looked upon marriage as the inevitable next step in their life cycle. Although Anna Kuthan hoped to travel and "see this country" before marriage, she gave up on those plans. Her fiancé was in a hurry "to get his own home" and insisted on an early wedding date. Anna reluctantly gave in but later conceded that "love is blind and marriage is a eyeopener."[57] However, even if the grand passion that girls hoped for never materialized, they at least wanted the independence to choose their mate.

In Eastern European shtetls, parents often relied on the marriage broker to arrange a match for their children. Without a voice, eligible girls waited with their dowries until a suitable groom was found. But new ideas of individual choice and free will, which gained ascendancy in the latter part of the nineteenth century, directly challenged the usefulness and the viability of the matchmaker; undercurrents of romantic love eroded the foundation of this shtetl custom. By the time of the great migration, matchmaking was already losing favor in the cities of Eastern Europe, and only a small minority of Jewish girls envisioned the shadchan-arranged marriage in America. Very traditional parents, however, still retained their faith in the services of the shadkhen and expressed shock over the notion that something as frivolous as romantic love should be the sole determinant of a match. When Lillian Wald mentioned her disapproval of arranged marriages to an Orthodox Jew, he erupted. "What . . . let a girl of seventeen, with no judgment whatsoever, decide on anything so important as a husband?"[58] Yet this is precisely

אַ בּוֹיטשִיק
אַפֿ טוּ דייט

A BOYCHIK
UP·TO·DATE

WORDS BY
L. GILROD
MUSIC BY
D. MEYROWITZ

SONG 50. VIOLIN 30.

New York
THEODORE LOHR
186 GRAND STREET

Left: America offered young men and women greater freedom to socialize. Above: This song features the "boychick," a dapper fellow dressed in swell clothing.

Vacations were a welcome respite from the daily routine of work.

what young women came to expect in America—the freedom to meet and spend time with boys on their own terms.

Young immigrants rebelled against the custom of matchmaking, arguing that marriage should not be reduced to a brokerage arrangement. Balking at such outside interference, they insisted that in America, it takes two, not three, to make a match. In 1903, the *Jewish Daily News* published an article entitled, "Troubles of Schadkhen" in which Schloime, who always has "an eye on the [case]" arranges a match between Sarah and Schmerel. Delighted with the shadkhen's choice, Schmerel showers his betrothed with expensive jewelry. But Sarah has other ideas: she rejects her suitor but keeps the watch and rings.[59] Such independence spelled the demise of matrimonial agents. In 1898 the *New York Tribune* interviewed one of these "Cupids of the Ghetto" and found that business was very bad indeed. Working out of his shop on Hester Street, the matchmaker had been forced to expand his business to letter-writing and teaching in order to make a living. Remembering better times, the shadkhen denounced the new practices of young Jews. "They learned how to start their own love affairs from the Americans, and it is one of the worst things they picked up. . . . The love which they have learned to put so much faith in dribbles out in trips to Coney [Island]. . . . In a month they are figuring out ways of getting rid of each other."[60]

But young immigrant Jews ignored such dire warnings. For them di goldene medina was the place of their romantic dreams where they would find their ideal lover.[61] Before she left Ukraine, fifteen-year-old Fannie Friedman dreamed about her new life in America. Anticipating that "my father's going to buy me some new clothes," she wondered, "Am I going to find a boyfriend there right away?"[62] As they reshaped their definitions of femininity to include American standards, so too did they rethink ideals of masculinity. Abraham Cahan wrote about these changing expectations in his 1902 account of a young girl who arrives at Ellis Island to meet her newly arrived sweetheart. Presenting him with a black derby hat, she insists that he put it on immediately. When the man protests, "Whoever wore a hat on week days?", she is quick to retort: "You must be an American nobleman, or I won't take you out of here. You don't think I'll walk through America with a peasant, do you?" Pointing to the hats she and her friends are sporting, she adds, "Why we are all ladies."[63] Although a Jewish immigrant girl's judgment was mediated by the realities of working-class experiences, her image of a "real catch" certainly differed from the shtetl cultural model.[64] "Modern" girls did not long for pious young scholars; instead, they dreamed of successful (or soon-to-be successful) husbands who would take them out of the ghetto.

But where to meet such a man? While mothers might ask relatives and friends to introduce their daughters to an appropriate suitor, young girls had different ideas. Looking for someone a "little special," they moved their mating game to the street. The neighborhood streets in immigrant communities served not only as corridors of consumption with the proliferation of peddlers and pushcarts but as social centers as well. Mothers would sit on their stoops to chat with neighbors, exchange news of home, and watch the passing scene of youth constantly in motion. Sara Abrams recalled that the streets of New York City were the theater of her youth. "We greatly appreciated the crowds in the street; we did not feel lonely one bit. We enjoyed seeing a parade on Fifth Avenue, as through it were a Grand Opera performance."[65]

Many Jewish immigrants transported the urban parade to a country setting. The burgeoning growth of summer resorts and hotels provided young girls with another opportunity to show off their stylishness. To participate a girl needed two things: fashionable clothing and a desire to meet men.[66] By the turn of the century, vacation spots had sprung up all over the country. Unlike the earlier watering holes that served the wealthy, places like the Catskills and South Haven, Michigan, catered to the needs of the middle and working classes. More than any other immigrant group, Jews embraced the notion of American vacationing in unprecedented numbers; by the 1890s, it was a normal expectation for all but the poorest Jews.[67] In response to the anti-Semitism of some gentile establishments that openly discriminated with signs such as "Hebrews Need Not Apply," Jewish innkeepers opened their own resorts.[68] In kosher hotels, boarding houses or farmhouses, Jewish "pleasureniks" relaxed together in the company of relatives and landsleit. Mothers often took their children away to the country to escape the sweltering city heat, and working girls saved all year to afford two weeks of "country, vacation, and fellows."[69] In these new "marriage arenas," dress was a major preoccupation. For married women, fashion was part of the social competition; for their daughters, stylish clothing opened the door to romantic adventure. Under a mother's encouraging eye, Jewish girls min-

Left and opposite: In their bathing suits and summer frocks, young women let their hair down on vacation at the beach.

gled with potential mates in the "strolling paths, the bathing places, and the dining rooms."[70] Wearing straw boaters, woolen bathing suits, and floral muslin dresses, daughters sought out the good times while their mothers looked on from the veranda.

But ambitious girls looking to pair off with an eligible "gent" first had to find him. An 1897 article bemoaning the lack of eligible men at summer resorts advertised "More Men Wanted." The author offers his sympathy to the "poor mammas" who clothed their daughters in a fashionable wardrobe and brought them to the seashore and mountain "with the fond hope that they may somewhere, at some time during their stay 'catch on.'"[71] In 1902 the *Forward* reported that "there are twelve young girls to every boy in the Catskills."[72] The disproportionate number of women prompted young girls to scramble for male attention, and they often relied on dress to gain that critical edge. Envisioning their two-week stay as a "coming-out party," working girls readied their vacation wardrobe weeks in advance. Elizabeth Hasanovitz reported:

> They sit up late into the night making dresses, petticoats, and useless cheap fineries; for they must appear "swell." . . . And, who knows? Fate may bring them together with a decent fellow. . . . So the long, exhausting deprivations, the investment in good clothes, may after all prove profitable.[73]

A girl looking for a little adventure, however, did not have to wait for a summer vacation. Turn-of-the-century urbanites had their pick of inexpensive commercial entertainment, and these popular amusements offered myriad opportunities to informally meet a "swell." America was undergoing a leisure revolution at the turn of the century, and immigrants found themselves in a world of recreation that promised social adventure, entertainment, and pleasure. Dr. Clara Rosenberg recalled that after her family had been in this country for several weeks her mother said that "there's [something] . . . about America I don't understand. What does it mean when everybody says 'Let's have fun.'"[74] While older Jews struggled with the concept, their children set out to find it. Girls with little spending money often relied on generous boyfriends to treat them.[75] Eighteen-year-old Mollie knew the limits of her small salary as a machine operator and counted on favors from men. "I guess if anyone wants to take me to a dance he won't have to ask me twice," she declared.[76]

Working girls joined the parade at the end of the workday. When the final bell rang, girls took a quick look in the mirror to apply another dusting of powder. Then, pulling elaborate hats from hooks on factory walls and securing them to their pompadours, girls escaped the stagnant air of crowded workrooms and the pressures of the job. But instead of hurrying home to join their families, girls gossiped with friends and lingered with boys on street corners. Groups came together informally, and men and women paired off to share a soda and have a good time.[77]

In contrast to the rigid barriers erected between unmarried men and women in the Old World, recreation in the New World encouraged the sexes to socialize together in public. At theaters, amusement parks, movies, and public dance halls young people came together to mingle, dance, and "play for a while."[78] Unfettered by the old restrictions, they flirted with each other and experimented with changing sex roles. Although Gertrude Yellin loved to socialize with her Russian friends and remembers dancing all night, she found the new rules confusing. "I didn't know how to go around with men," Gertrude said. "I was brought up in a religious home and . . . you just keep away. You don't know how to kiss, you don't know how to flirt."[79] As they navigated their way through the twists and turns of modern courtship, immigrants improvised behavior, following the lead of their more experienced

peers. Minnie Laken remembers encouraging her boyfriend to take her to Coney Island and Russian Balls. "I used to tell him, 'You have to learn it. . . . When you are here you have to be like they live here.'"[80]

This is not to say that older women eschewed commercial entertainment. To the contrary, introduction to American recreation was an important rite of passage for every immigrant. Viola Paradise, for instance, reported that "as soon as her relatives have bought her some American clothes," they take the newcomer to the nickel show where she hears "Yiddish jokes . . . and American popular music, and she marvels at the moving-pictures."[81] It is clear that Jewish women of all ages shared an interest "in the world of urban products and pleasures" as a temporary escape from tenement life.[82] But young girls brought a different perspective to these experiences. Unlike Jewish immigrant mothers who eked out precious moments of leisure time to spend with their families, working girls struck out on their own delighting in the heady sensation of individual freedom. Russian-born Molly Chernikovsky came to America alone in 1909 at the

Couples danced cheek to cheek at a Jewish Community Center dance in Chicago.

Opposite: A roller coaster at Riverview Park. Said one immigrant about urban pleasures: "We sang. . . . We danced. . . . We had a life."

age of thirteen to join her siblings. Working as seamstresses in a Philadelphia factory, Molly and her friends explored the pleasures of the city. "We went on Sundays to Fairmount Park. We packed a big meal. We sang. We danced Russian dances. . . . We had a life."[82] In these contained environments of social permissiveness, young people seized the opportunity to pursue their new status as Americans.

All of these urban pleasures fueled a young girl's interest in dress, coalescing the promise of consumption with romantic fantasies. As girls signaled their desire to participate in America's playground, they dressed with one eye on fashion and the other on boys. According to reformer Belle Israels, it was a simple equation. The girl attracts the boy, and "he spends the money."[84] Many young female immigrants interpreted new clothing as a practical and worthwhile investment in their future.[85] When interviewed about the practices of his employees, a shop owner reported, "There isn't a girl here that doesn't expect to marry before long, and she puts what she makes on her back, because a fellow naturally goes for the best-looking and best-dressed girl."[86]

This preoccupation with dress and blatant display of physical charms must have taken some mothers aback. Appearance received little attention in the Old Country as a criterion for matchmaking. Indeed, some grooms met their brides for the first time under the wedding canopy. But the new rules of romantic love placed a high premium on attractiveness.[87] Dressing up became a way to gain attention, a beguiling invitation to look. This public presentation of self was about more than hormones, however; it was about status. Young people wanted to locate themselves in American society, and clothing offered the most visible marker. By appropriating the symbols of material abundance, they announced their cultural flexibility and their hopes for assimilation.[88] In her memoirs, Sara Abrams described a scene at the Yid-

Above: Riverview Amusement Park.

Left: Young woman in white lace-trimmed dress. Opposite: Bessie Adler's bridal portrait.

dish theater where the clothing in the audience overshadowed the costumes on the stage.

> Everyone wore their holiday clothes. . . . Shidichem (match-making) were often the excuse for urging young man or young woman to buy a ticket . . . so that possible mates could see you. . . . No item of wearing apparel was overlooked, and in the case of the young lady, she was sure to wear her best. . . . Diamond rings and scarf-pins were sported by the young men, as evidence of their affluence.[89]

Clothes, money, boys, and freedom. What were mothers to make of this vortex of changes that pulled at family ties? Raised in one culture, they now found themselves in another. Proud of their children's advancement, they also felt the pain of their rejection. As they watched their children jettison so much of their heritage to become American women, mothers might have worried that the bonds between themselves and their daughters might be permanently severed. But they would be wrong. The struggles were real and painful, but this was the social revolt of adolescents. As Leslie

Tentler so convincingly argues, while the social life of working girls conferred a great deal of personal freedom, it ultimately reinforced conservative ideas of femininity.[90] For all of their rebelliousness, young girls envisioned their social independence as temporary, and they defined adult achievement in terms of marriage and a family. Schooled in matrimony, daughters inevitably joined their mothers in the sphere of domestic life.

As they made the transition from a single to a married life, girls rediscovered their emotional center. Rebellious adolescents might scoff at their mother's inability to talk about hemlines or hairstyles, but new brides looked up to their mothers as the best teachers of survival strategies and domestic resourcefulness. It was easier to detect a parent's soothing virtues and daily sacrifices from the vantage point of adulthood. As Jews established themselves in America, both financially and culturally, older women began to tie their own self-fulfillment to consumerism. They used dress as a display of luxury that expressed social aspirations, just as their daughters used dress to express social independence.

This is not to say that the generational gulf disappeared or that children ultimately decided to recreate the world of their elders. A rite of passage could not erase the cultural conflicts of tradition and modernity, custom and assimilation, and understanding and confusion that demanded the immigrants' attention.[91] The barriers that children and parents erected were real, and the choices they made reflected very different circumstances. But if saying "I do" does not change the person, it does alter the person's perspective. As they took on the responsibilities of their own children's well-being, many young Jewish women sifted through the complexities of intermingled destinies. As Mollie Linker said when asked to tell the story of her own immigration experience, "I think the whole story is about my mother."[92]

Left: As a young woman walked from the chuppah, it was her mother's world she was approaching.

Notes

1. Paula E. Hyman, "Gender and the Immigrant Jewish Experience in the United States," in Judith R. Baskin, ed., *Jewish Women in Historical Perspective* (Detroit: 1991), 223.

2. Susan A. Glenn, *Daughters of the Shtetl: Life and Labor in the Immigrant Generation* (Ithaca: 1990), 48.

3. "The Economic Situation of the Jewish Woman, Part I: The Woman in the Shop," *Di Froyen-Velt*, July 1913, 14.

4. Maxine Seller, ed., *Immigrant Women* (Philadelphia: 1981), 124.

5. Elizabeth Ewen, *Immigrant Women in the Land of Dollars: Life and Culture on the Lower East Side, 1890–1925* (New York: 1985), 188.

6. Viola Paradise, "The Jewish Immigrant Girl in Chicago," *Survey*, September 6, 1913, 704.

7. Fannie Shoock, Ellis Island Oral History Project, Ellis Island Immigration Museum.

8. Margaret Mead Papers, Research in Contemporary Cultures, G45, v. 5, J-R 113, December 7–8, 1947, Library of Congress.

9. Dr. Morris Moel, Ellis Island Oral History Project.

10. Belle L. Mead,"The Social Pleasures of East Side Jews," (master's thesis, Columbia University, 1904), 3.

11. Elizabeth Hasanovitz, *One of Them: Chapters from a Passionate Autobiography* (Boston: 1918), 42.

12. Leah Asher, "The Old-Fashioned Mother and the American Girl," *Jewish Daily News*, August 22, 1902.

13. Lillian Wald, *House on Henry Street* (1915; reprint, New York: 1971), 253.

14. J. Pfeffer, "The Two Generations," trans. C. Markowitz, *Jewish Daily News*, July 21, 1902.

15. Anzia Yezierska, *Hungry Hearts* (Chicago: 1920), 201.

16. Estelle Belford, Ellis Island Oral History Project.

17. Ivan Chermayeff, Fred Wasserman, and Mary J. Shapiro, *Ellis Island: An Illustrated History of the Immigrant Experience* (New York: 1991), 70.

18. Corinne Azen Krause, "Urbanization Without Breakdown: Italian, Jewish, and Slavic Immigrant Women in Pittsburgh, 1900–1945," *Journal of Urban History*, 4(3) (May 1978): 291–306.

19. Irving Howe and Kenneth Libo, *How We Lived: A Documentary History of Immigrant Jews in America* (New York: 1979), 319.

20. *Forward*, August 8, 1905, quoted in Howe and Libo, *How We Lived*, 139.

21. Sally Goldstein, interview with Carla Reiter and Joanne Grossman, March 3, 1993.

22. Sara J. Abrams, "Things Trivial," American Jewish Autobiographies Collection, #92, YIVO Archives, YIVO Institute for Jewish Research.

23. Margaret Mead Papers, Research in Contemporary Cultures, G45, v. 5, J-R 113, December 8, 1947.

24. Sophonisba P. Breckinridge, *New Homes for Old* (New York: 1921), 172–73.

25. Fred Davis, *Fashion, Culture, and Identity* (Chicago: 1992), 27.

26. "Autobiography of a Shop Girl," *Frank Leslie's Popular Monthly*, 61 (May 1903): 58.

27. Neil M. Cowan and Ruth Schwartz Cowan, *Our Parents' Lives: The Americanization of Eastern European Jews* (New York: 1989), 71.

28. Sydney Stahl Weinberg, "Jewish Mothers and Immigrant Daughters: Positive and Negative Role Models," *Journal of American Ethnic History,* 6(2) (Spring 1987): 50.

29. Ida Feldman, Ellis Island Oral History Project.

30. Sadie Frowne, "The Story of a Sweatshop Girl," in Leon Stein and Philip Taft, eds., *Workers Speak: Self Portraits* (New York: 1971), 118.

31. Sue Ainslie Clark and Edith Wyatt, *Making Both Ends Meet: The Income and Outlay of New York Working Girls* (New York: 1911), 24.

32. Marcus Ravage, *An American Dream in the Making* (New York: 1917), reprinted in Howe and Libo, *How We Lived*, 5.

33. Ewen, *Immigrant Women in the Land of Dollars*, 26.

34. Sydelle Kramer and Jenny Masur, eds., *Jewish Grandmothers* (Boston: 1976), 130.

35. Kathy Peiss, *Cheap Amusements: Working Women and Leisure in Turn-of-the-Century New York* (New York: 1986), 62–66.

36. Wald, *The House on Henry Street*, 190.

37. "Just Between Ourselves, Girls," *Jewish Daily News*, December 14, 1902.

38. Hasanovitz, *One of Them*, 227.

39. Sydney Stahl Weinberg, *The World of Our Mothers: The Lives of Jewish Immigrant Women* (Chapel Hill: 1988), 94.

40. Angela Partington, "Popular Fashion and Working-Class Affluence," in Juliet Ash and Elizabeth Wilson, eds., *Chic Thrills: A Fashion Reader* (California: 1993), 150.

41. Jane Addams, "Some Reflections on the Failure of the Modern City to Provide Recreation for Young Girls," *Charities*, 21 (December 5, 1908): 365–68.

42. *New York Evening Journal*, November 26, 1909, quoted in Glenn, *Daughters of the Shtetl*, 165.

43. Hasanovitz, *One of Them*, 310.

44. Mina K. Friedman, "Time About No News To All," unpublished manuscript, courtesy of Alan Friedman.

45. Judith Smith, *Family Connections: A History of Italian & Jewish Immigrant Lives in Providence Rhode Island 1900–1940* (Albany: 1985), 61.

46. Elisabeth Howe Bliss, "Intimate Study of Fifty Working Girls," (master's thesis, Columbia University, 1915), 74–76.

47. Ewen, *Immigrant Women in the Land of Dollars*, 106.

48. Frowne, "The Story of a Sweatshop Girl," 118.

49. Robert Coit Chapin, *The Standard Living Among Workingmen's Families in New York City* (New York: 1909), 164.

50. Breckenridge, *New Homes for Old*, 137.

51. Sydney Stahl Weinberg, "Jewish Mothers and Immigrant Daughters," 45.

52. Margaret Mead Papers, Research in Contemporary Cultures, G45, v. 5, J-R 113, December 7–8, 1947.

53. Tape I-134, New York City Immigrant Labor History Project.

54. Leslie Woodcock Tentler, *Wage-Earning Women: Industrial Work and Family Life in the United States 1900–1930* (New York: 1979), 60–62.

55. Tape I-59, New York City Immigrant Labor History Project.

56. Bliss, "Intimate Studies in the Lives of Fifty Working Girls," 38.

57. Interview with Anna Kuthan, New York City Immigrant Labor History Project.

58. Wald, *The House on Henry Street*, 216.

59. Wm. Heller, "Troubles of a Schadchen," *Jewish Daily News*, June 17, 1903.

60. "Schadchens Find Business Bad," *New York Tribune*, January 9, 1898, in Allon Schoener, ed., *Portal to America: The Lower East Side, 1870–1925* (New York: 1967), 117–118.

61. Alice Kessler Harris, Introduction to Anzia Yezierska, *Bread Givers* (Garden City, New York: 1925; reprint, New York: 1975), vii.

62. Fannie Friedman, Ellis Island Oral History Project.

63. Abraham Cahan, "All Right! Hurry Up!," in Moses Rischin, ed., *Grandma Never Lived in America: The New Journalism of Abraham Cahan* (Bloomington: 1985), 147.

64. Peiss, *Cheap Amusements*, 66.

65. Abrams, "Things Trivial."

66. Ewen, *Immigrant Women in the Land of Dollars*, 209.

67. Andrew R. Heinze, *Adapting to Abundance: Jewish Immigrants, Mass Consumption, and the Search for American Identity* (New York: 1990), 127.

68. "Michigan Summer Resorts Bar Jews," *Sentinel*, July 3, 1914.

69. Hasanovitz, *One of Them*, 227.

70. New York *Morgen Zhurnal*, May 9, 1907, quoted in Heinze, *Adapting to Abundance*, 130.

71. William Alyn Watt, "The Summer Girl," *American Jewess*, July 1897, 175–76.

72. *Forward*, August 9, 1904, reprinted in Howe and Libo, *How We Lived*, 78.

73. Hasanovitz, *One of Them*, 247.

74. Dr. Clara Rosenberg, Ellis Island Oral History Project.

75. Kathy Peiss examines the practice of "treating" in meticulous detail in *Cheap Amusement: Working Women and Leisure in Turn-of-the-Century New York* (Philadelphia: 1986).

76. Bliss, "Intimate Studies in the Lives of Fifty Working Girls," 38.

77. Kathy Peiss, "Leisure and the 'Woman Question'" in Richard Butsch, ed., *For Fun and Profit: The Transformation of Leisure into Consumption* (Philadelphia: 1990), 107–11.

78. "The Public Dance Halls of the Lower East Side," *The Jewish Daily News*, May 15, 1902.

79. Gertrude Yellin, Ellis Island Oral History Project.

80. Minnie Laken, Ellis Island Oral History Project.

81. Paradise, "The Jewish Immigrant Girl in Chicago," 701.

82. Glenn, *Daughters of the Shtetl*, 162.

83. Charlotte Baum, Paula Hyman and Sonya Michel, *The Jewish Woman in America* (New York: 1975), 96.

84. Belle Linder Israels, "Diverting a Pastime," *Leslie's Illustrated Weekly*, July 17, 1911, 94.

85. Doris Weatherford, *Foreign & Female: Immigrant Women in America, 1840–1930* (New York: 1986), 98.

86. Helen Campbell, *Prisoners of Poverty: Women Wage-Workers, Their Trades and Their Lives* (Boston: 1887; reprint, Westport, Conn.:1970), 175.

87. Baum, et. al., *The Jewish Woman in America*, 222–23.

88. Heinze, *Adapting to Abundance*, 5–8.

89. Abrams, "Things Trivial."

90. Tentler, *Wage-Earning Women*, 60–62.

91. Ewen, *Immigrant Women in the Land of Dollars*, 266.

92. Kramer and Masur, *Jewish Grandmothers*, 91.

Illustration Credits

Introduction

ix, Mr. and Mrs. Newton N. Minow; 1, Mr. and Mrs. Newton N. Minow; 2, Michele Vishny; 3, Louise N. Mages; 4, Mr. and Mrs. Leonard Cohen; 5, Mr. and Mrs. Newton N. Minow; 7, Mr. and Mrs. Richard D. Abelson; 8, Louise N. Mages; 9 top, Paula A. Golden; 9 bottom, Dr. and Mrs. Herman L. Eisenberg; 10 top, Chicago Jewish Archives/Spertus Institute; 10 bottom, CHS, ICHi-23930; 12, New York Public Library; 13, New York Public Library; 14, Michele Vishny.

Di Alte Heym

16–17, Chicago Jewish Archives/Spertus Institute; 18 top, Marilyn D. Davis; 18 bottom, Mr. and Mrs. Newton N. Minow; 19 left, Mr. and Mrs. Leonard Cohen; 19 right top and bottom, *Life in the Shtetl* (1986); 20, top, Sarah Miller Rovner; 20, bottom, cake mold, Julia Mann Gershon, Harry Mann, and John Mann; mortar and pestle, Nina Reiter; copper pot, Jewish Historical Society of Maryland, Inc.; washing cup, Lois and Richard Janger; 21, YIVO Institute for Jewish Research; 22, YIVO Institute for Jewish Research; 23 left, The Family of Charles and Shirley Marovitz; 23 right, Elaine G. Rosen and Dina Weisman Rosen; 24 top, YIVO Institute for Jewish Research; 24 bottom, *Life in the Shtetl* (1986); 25 top left, candlesticks, Vivian S. (Mrs. Bernard L.) Pava; two cloths, Julia Mann Gershon, Harry Mann, and John Mann; 25 top right, Elaine G. Rosen and Dina Weisman Rosen; 25 bottom, Sanford L. Aronin; 26 top and bottom, YIVO Institute for Jewish Research; 27, YIVO Institute for Jewish Research; 28 top, Jewish Historical Society of Maryland, Inc.; 28 bottom, YIVO Institute for Jewish Research; 29, shawls: top, Belle Biondi; middle, Roberta Gottlieb Cogen; bottom, Annette A. Grafman; 30 top, YIVO Institute for Jewish Research; 30 bottom, Shirley Silvers; 31, YIVO Institute for Jewish Research; 32, Gloria Meiselman Stern; 33 top, Muriel Golman; 33 bottom, Myrna K. Metz; 34 top, Marcia Rustin Kraut; 34 bottom, *Life in the Shtetl* (1986); 35 front, kiddish cups, The Forest Group (The Janger Family Collection); 35 middle, matzo cover, Ruth Fairfield; 35 back, candlesticks, Lois and Richard Janger; 36, Abraham J. Karp, Deborah B. Karp, and Gertrude Feldbaum; 37, Naomi and William Rushakoff; 38 top, Boston Public Library; 38 bottom, YIVO Institute for Jewish Research; 39, YIVO Institute for Jewish Research; 40, YIVO Institute for Jewish Research; 41, Immigrant City Archives; 42, YIVO Institute for Jewish Research; 43 top, Immigrant City Archives; 43 bottom, YIVO Institute for Jewish Research; 44–45, Marilyn Golden; 45 right, shawl, amber beads, and travel clock, Rebecca Anne Sive; pillow, Rose Dick Wandel; candlesticks, Naomi and William Rushakoff.

They Don't Wear Wigs Here

48–49, CHS, ICHi-04191; 50, Elaine G. Rosen and Dina Weisman Rosen; 51 left, Marilyn D. Davis; 51 top right, Annette A. Grafman; 51 bottom right, Collection of John and Selma Appel, Michigan State University Museum; 52 top, YIVO Institute for Jewish Research; 52 bottom, Mr. and Mrs. Richard D. Abelson; 53, Marilyn Golden; 54, Museum of the City of New York; 56 top and bottom, Northwestern University Library, Special Collections; 57 left, Northwestern University Library, Special Collections; 57 top right, Mr. and Mrs. Richard D. Abelson; 57 bottom right, Abraham J. Karp, Deborah B. Karp, and Gertrude Feldbaum; 58, Judy L. Dean and Susan Dean Jacobs; 59, YIVO Institute for Jewish Research; 60, Marilyn Golden; 61, hats: left, Shelly Farber Marks; middle, Jewish Historical Society of Maryland,

Inc.; right, CHS Costume Collection; 61 bottom, The Family of Charles and Shirley Marovitz; 62, Mr. and Mrs. Richard D. Abelson; 63 top, Lynn Historical Society and Museum; 63 bottom left, Museum of Jewish Heritage; 63 bottom right, CHS Costume Collection; 64 top, Myrna K. Metz; 64 bottom, CHS Costume Collection; 65, YIVO Institute for Jewish Research; 67 top, Chicago Jewish Archives/ Spertus Institute; 67 bottom, CHS, ICHi-20244; 68, New York Public Library; 69, Chicago Jewish Archives/Spertus Institute; 71, from *A. M. Rothschild's Catalog* (Spring and Summer 1900), CHS Library; 72–73 CHS, DN 4000; 74, CHS, ICHi-20239; 75 top and bottom, Museum of the City of New York; 77, Library of Congress; 78 top, CHS, CRC144B; 78 bottom, Immigrant City Archives; 79, The Family of Fay Kanter Cooper; 80, Carol B. White.

Color Plates

84, hats: left, Shelly Farber Marks; middle, Jewish Historical Society of Maryland, Inc.; right, CHS Costume Collection; 84 bottom left, Elizabeth S. Brown; 84 bottom right, Abraham J. Karp, Deborah B. Karp, and Gertrude Feldbaum; 85, Ruth F. Appel; 86, The Family of Fay Kanter Cooper; 87, Louise N. Mages; 88, The Family of Fay Kanter Cooper; 89, Mrs. Harold (Bunny) Kohn.

Greening Out

90-91, Collection of John and Selma Appel, Michigan State University Museum; 92, American Jewish Historical Society; 93, Immigrant City Archives; 94, Carpenter Center, Harvard University; 95, Chicago Jewish Archives/Spertus Institute; 96, *from Ellis Island: An Illustrated History of the Immigrant Experience* (1991); 97, YIVO Institute for Jewish Research; 98, Mr. and Mrs. Richard D. Abelson; 99, Julia Mann Gershon, Harry Mann, and John Mann; 100 top, CHS Costume Collection; 100 bottom, Immigrant City Archives; 101, Boston Public Library; 102–103, New York Public Library; 105 top, Museum of the City of New York; 105 bottom, New York Public Library; 106, Museum of the City of New York; 107, Chicago Jewish Archives/Spertus Institute; 108 top, New York Public Library; 108 bottom, Esther Hirsch; 109, New York Public Library; 111, CHS Prints and Photographs Collection; 112, Library of Congress; 114, YIVO Institute for Jewish Research; 116, left and right, CHS Costume Collection.

Mothers and Daughters

120, Mr. and Mrs. Richard D. Abelson; 121, Marilyn Golden; 122 top, Chicago Jewish Archives/Spertus Institute; 122 bottom, The Family of Fay Kanter Cooper; 123, The Family of Charles and Shirley Marovitz; 124, Carpenter Center, Harvard University; 125, Marilyn Golden; 127 top, New-York Historical Society; 127 bottom, CHS, ICHi-20256; 128 top, Judy L. Dean and Susan Dean Jacobs; 128 bottom, New York Public Library; 129, YIVO Institute for Jewish Research; 130 top, Chicago Jewish Archives/Spertus Institute; 130 bottom, The Family of Charles and Shirley Marovitz; 131, New York Public Library; 132, Mr. and Mrs. Leonard Cohen; 133, Chicago Jewish Archives/Spertus Institute; 134, Alan H. Friedman; 135, New-York Historical Society; 136 top, Carol B. White; 136 bottom, Louise N. Mages; 137, Mr. and Mrs. Leonard Cohen; 138 left, Chicago Jewish Archives/Spertus Institute; 138 right, American Jewish Historical Society; 139, University of Illinois at Chicago, Special Collections; 140, Chicago Jewish Archives/Spertus Institute; 141, top and bottom, Louise N. Mages; 142, YIVO Institute for Jewish Research; 143, CHS, DN 64,657; 144 top, CHS, ICHi-23572; 144 bottom, Mr. and Mrs. Newton N. Minow; 145, Judy L. Dean and Susan Dean Jacobs; 146, Mr. and Mrs. Richard D. Abelson.

Index

Illustrations are indicated in italics. If a subject is discussed and illustrated on the same page, the illustration is not separately indicated.